NEW TESTAMENT APOCALYPTIC

INTERPRETING BIBLICAL TEXTS

The Gospels, Fred B. Craddock

New Testament Apocalyptic Literature, Paul S. Minear

The Pentateuch, Lloyd R. Bailey

INTERPRETING **ibt** BIBLICAL TEXTS

New Testament Apocalyptic

Paul S. Minear

LLOYD R. BAILEY
and
VICTOR PAUL FURNISH
EDITORS

ABINGDON   NASHVILLE

NEW TESTAMENT APOCALYPTIC

Copyright © 1981 by Abingdon

Library of Congress Cataloging in Publication Data

MINEAR, PAUL SEVIER, 1906-
New Testament apocalyptic
(Interpreting Biblical texts)
Bibliography: p.
  1. Apocalyptic literature. 2. Bible. N.T.—Criticism, interpretation,
  etc. I. Title. II. Series.
BS 646.M55   228'.06   81-4721

ISBN 0-687-27890-2   AACR2

MANUFACTURED BY THE PARTHENON PRESS AT
NASHVILLE, TENNESSEE, UNITED STATES OF AMERICA

INTERPRETING BIBLICAL TEXTS:
Editors' Foreword

The volumes in this series have been planned for those who are convinced that the Bible has meaning for our life today, and who wish to enhance their skills as interpreters of the biblical texts. Such interpreters must necessarily engage themselves in two closely related tasks: (1) determining as much as possible about the original meaning of the various biblical writings, and (2) determining in what respect these texts are still meaningful today. The objective of the present series is to keep both of these tasks carefully in view, and to provide assistance in relating the one to the other.

Because of this overall objective it would be wrong to regard the individual volumes in this series as commentaries, as homiletical expositions of selected texts, or as abstract discussions of "the hermeneutical problem." Rather, they have been written in order to identify and illustrate what is involved in relating the meaning of the biblical texts in their own times to their meaning in ours. Biblical commentaries and other technical reference works sometimes focus exclusively on the first, paying little or no attention to the second. On the other hand, many attempts to expound the contemporary "relevance" of biblical themes or passages pay scant attention to the intentions of the texts themselves. And although one of the standard topics of "hermeneutics" is how a text's original meaning relates to its present meaning, such discussions often employ highly technical philosophical language and proceed with little reference to concrete examples. By way of contrast, the present volumes are written in language that will be understood by scholars, clergy and laypersons alike, and they deal with concrete texts, actual problems of interpretation, and practical procedures for moving from "then" to "now."

Each contributor to this series is committed to three basic tasks: (1) a description of the salient features of the particular type of biblical literature or section of the canon assigned to him; (2) the identification and explanation of the basic assumptions that guide his analysis and explication of those materials; and (3) the discussion of possible contemporary meanings of representative texts, in view of the specified assumptions with which the interpreter approaches them. Considerations that should be borne in mind by the interpreter in reflecting upon contemporary meanings of these texts are introduced by the sign ● and are accentuated with a different size of type.

The assumptions that are brought to biblical interpretation may vary from one author to the next, and will undoubtedly differ from those of many readers. Nonetheless, we believe that the present series, by illustrating how careful interpreters carry out their tasks, will encourage readers to be more reflective about the way they interpret the Bible.

Lloyd Bailey
Duke Divinity School

Victor Paul Furnish
Perkins School of Theology
Southern Methodist University

ACKNOWLEDGMENTS

For half a century I have been puzzling over the problems considered in this book. Accordingly, it is impossible to register all the debts I have incurred over so long a period. I must, however, mention several. I am grateful for the hospitality of the faculty of Southern Baptist Theological Seminary in Louisville, where material from the first three chapters was used in the Gheens Lectures for 1979. I recall also with appreciation the stimulus received from students in a seminar at Emory University in 1980. Much cogent editorial advice has been received from Victor P. Furnish, one of the editors of this series. If a dedicatory page were permitted, it would bear the names of Leander E. Keck and J. Louis Martyn, former students whose friendship over the years has been a source of great delight and who represent many other students from whom I have not ceased to learn. As always I have benefited greatly from the discerning eye and wise counsel of my wife.

Paul S. Minear

CONTENTS

PREFACE   **11**

APOCALYPTIC PROPHECY AND CHARISMATIC
GIFTS

1   **THE GIFT TO THE PROPHET**   **15**
2   **THE GIFT TO THE CONGREGATION**   **33**
3   **THE HORIZONS OF APOCALYPTIC PROPHECY**   **48**

PROPHETIC VISIONS AND CONGREGATIONAL
DISCERNMENT

4   **A VISION OF HEAVEN**   **67**
    (Revelation 4:1–8:1)
5   **THE DISCERNMENT OF THE SPIRIT**
    IN BAPTISM   **78**
    (1 Peter)
6   **A VISION OF HEAVENLY WARFARE**   **91**
    (Revelation 11:19–14:5)

7 THE DISCERNMENT OF THE SPIRIT
   IN SHARED FUTILITY   102
   (Romans 8)
8 A VISION OF THE DEATH OF DEATH   115
   (Revelation 19:11–21:4)
9 THE DISCERNMENT OF VICTORY
   OVER DEATH   126
   (Hebrews 2:1–4:13)
10 A VISION OF THE HOLY CITY   135
   (Revelation 21:9–22:9)
11 THE DISCERNMENT OF LIFE IN THE CITY   144
   (Hebrews 12:1–13:25)

AIDS FOR THE INTERPRETER   153

PREFACE

There are many reasons why the problems addressed in this book should not be shrugged off as obsolete or as problems that are of concern only to professional academicians. Some of those reasons inhere in the fact that apocalyptic patterns of thought are central within the New Testament itself. Christian churches continue to treat that Testament as a book which in some sense exerts an authority for determining their basic beliefs and duties. Because this literature is itself thoroughly pervaded by the perspectives of apocalyptic prophecy, failures to penetrate those perspectives will guarantee that the churches misunderstand their mandate and mission. And such a guarantee has, I believe, been amply demonstrated long since. To the degree, then, that Christians are loyal to their scriptural base, to that degree do they obligate themselves to improve their ways of interpreting New Testament apocalyptic.

Concern with the problems addressed in this book also emerges from current situations in American society. In countless places and under diverse conditions, charismatic gifts have erupted with explosive force, filling some Christians with spiritual ecstasy, bewildering others with their manifest power, and alienating still others with their apparently demonic excesses. Whether these activities take the form of speaking with tongues, demon-exorcism, faith-healing, or prophecy—whether they appear surrounded by the melodramatic trappings of a TV spectacular or during quite unspectacular prayers within a tiny house-church—they are almost always viewed as a recurrence of Pentecostal gifts (as described in Acts 2 and 1 Corinthians 12–14). And almost always they are explained in terms of a modern apocalypticism that is viewed as a lineal descendant of the dominant world view in the New Testament. It is this eruption of charismatic gifts that impels thoughtful Christians, whether or not they have received such gifts, to reexamine their ways of interpreting New Testament apocalyptic.

APOCALYPTIC PROPHECY
AND
CHARISMATIC GIFTS

1 THE GIFT TO THE PROPHET

In its broadest sense, the word *apocalyptic* designates the disclosure through human agents of God's presence and activity, which otherwise would remain hidden from his people. Beginning with this broad definition, we trust that successive chapters will clarify more specific meanings.[1] In English the same term serves as both a noun and an adjective. As the latter, it may be used to accompany four different nouns. First of all, the adjective may be used to qualify a particular book, a form of literature, or a genre of speech, either oral or written. In the New Testament, the best example of this genre is the book of Revelation and the successive visions of which it is composed. In fact, behind the English noun in the title *Revelation* stands the Greek word *apokalypsis*. Indeed this same book is often called The Apocalypse. It is the occurrence of this word in the first verse of the book that has led to the use of this adjective to refer to other examples of the same genre.

The second use of the adjective is to qualify the noun *prophecy*. In the New Testament the clearest example of this

[1]See also the articles "Apocalypse, Genre" and "Apocalypticism" by Paul D. Hanson, *IDBSup*, pp. 27-34.

use is again provided by the book of Revelation, for John
preferred to call his writing a book of prophecy and to think
of himself as a prophet (1:3; 10:11; 22:6-19). Later readers
may say *apocalypse,* but John thought *prophecy;* we should
follow his example so far as possible. Although his reports of
visions were clearly apocalyptic in form, they were an
integral part of his vocation as a prophet. To be sure,
distinctions may be drawn among various kinds of prophecies. For example, concerning Agabus'[2] prediction of famine
for Jerusalem Christians (Acts 11:27-30), there is perhaps no
need to call such a prophecy apocalyptic in form; the term is
more in order when dealing with such a remark as that of
Jesus: "I saw Satan fall like lightning from heaven" (Luke
10:18). We may say that not all early Christian prophets were
apocalyptists in the form of their utterance, but it is more
important to recognize that all apocalyptists in the New
Testament were prophets in the character of their vocation.
Therefore this book must deal with more than a single
literary genre; we must seek to comprehend the gift of
prophetic vocation. Chapters 4, 6, 8, and 10 concentrate on
this task.

The adjective can apply, however, to more than a specific
form of utterance and to more than the vocation of a limited
number of prophets. It can apply to patterns of thought that
were the stock-in-trade of those prophets, but which came to
be adopted by leaders of the churches who had not
themselves received this special charismatic gift. As a result
of the work of the chain of prophets—John the Baptist,
Jesus, the original band of apostles, the wider circle of
apostles including Paul and seers like John—one may speak

[2]Instead of Agabus, I might have mentioned as prophets the four
daughters of Philip (Acts 21:9). That would have shown that in the early
church this charismatic gift was not limited to one sex. So in the following
chapters when I speak of prophets I intend to include Christians of both
sexes.

of an apocalyptic mind-set or world-scape which in varying degrees shaped the thinking of virtually all members of the first generation church, including the non-prophetic authors of some of the writings in the New Testament. To use Amos Wilder's image, these patterns of thought provided the deeper "root-systems" that sustained the growing communities.

Finally, a fourth noun, *movement,* may be modified by the adjective apocalyptic. In its nascent form, Christianity was such a movement. Its origins cannot be explained apart from those root-systems. It received its sense of vocation, its sense of its own distinctive purposes, from the visions of its prophets. In chapters 5, 7, 9, and 11, we will seek to illustrate these last two uses of the term apocalyptic.

To sum up, then, we will move from accounts of prophetic visions that constitute a distinctive literary genre toward a treatment of the shared vocation of prophet and church. Whether dealing with the narrower target of a specific vision or the broader target of an apocalyptic movement, we will be exploring the mysteries of a vocation defined as a continuing dialogue between heaven and earth. It is the character of that dialogue which poses the salient difficulties in interpreting apocalyptic in any of its four phases.

A second term that elicits confusion is the term *charismatic* (or *spiritual*) *gifts.* Quite normally the New Testament speaks of prophecy as such a gift. The first point to stress is the vast variety of activities indicated by this specific gift. John the Baptist should not be overlooked, with his symbolic break with conventional manners, his announcement of coming judgment, his call to the wilderness. Jesus must be included, with his sayings and signs, his appeal to his nation as a prophet like Moses (Acts 3:22). All the gifts imparted to the apostles by the risen Lord belong within the scope of reference. When a person says "charismatic gifts" it is well to take such prophets as these as the standard by which to measure other gifts. Let us take two examples at this point; others will follow later.

The gift of the Spirit came to John in such a way as to impel him to say, "I was in the Spirit on the Lord's day, and I heard behind me a loud voice like a trumpet, saying, 'Write what you see . . . (Rev 1:10). His instructions from the risen Lord led him to conclude each of his letters to the churches with the injunction: "If you have an ear, listen to what the Spirit is saying to the churches" (3:6; my own translation).[3]

A second example is Paul, writing to the church in Corinth. He claimed to have received "the Spirit which is from God." Through that Spirit, he said, "God has revealed to us . . . what no eye has seen, nor ear heard, nor the heart of man conceived." This revelation enabled the apostolic prophet to impart a secret and hidden wisdom of God in words not taught by human wisdom but taught by the Spirit. Paul was fully aware that God's wisdom was foolishness to men and that God's power was weakness to men. (Of that the Cross was evidence enough.) Yet he believed that his readers in Corinth had been taught by the same Spirit so that they could spiritually discern "the gifts bestowed on us by God" (1 Corinthians 2). Both Paul and John thought of the Spirit as the single source of the twin gifts of prophecy and discernment. It was when these twin gifts converged that a congregation was enabled to hear the word of the Lord and to see his works.

Some modern confusions over spiritual gifts would be dispelled if Christians continued to think of Paul and John as the prime exemplars of prophecy and if the Cross of Christ remained an effective index of the wisdom and power that are communicated by the Holy Spirit. It is a quite different

[3]John traced the gift of the Spirit not alone to his own listening and writing but to the churches' action of listening and obeying as well.

range of phenomena that comes to mind when we read in current literature references to charismatic speech. Some minds gravitate to political matters and visualize a spell-casting politician who can arouse a public audience to great excitement during an election campaign. For others the word *charismatic* calls into memory a popular television evangelist who has demonstrated the power to heal the sick or to decode scriptural predictions concerning the end of the world. Still others rest their hopes for the renewal of the church on the recent upsurge of speaking in tongues and ecstatic praying. As we seek to recover the character of apocalyptic prophecy we must not transfer any of these current understandings of spiritual gifts back to the biblical stage. The eagerness to identify modern experience with ancient is one of the obstacles to our quest.

Undoubtedly, one of the problems to surmount when interpreting New Testament apocalyptic is the vast cultural chasm between the ancient, agrarian, Oriental society and the technocratic society of the modern, Western world. We should welcome all methods of study that help us reduce the distortions due to this chasm. Gerd Theissen, for example, reminds us of the degree to which the earliest churches were characterized by three features.[4] First of all, those communities accorded supreme status and authority to the charismatic revealer of divine secrets, the risen Jesus, who was felt to be present among them in a mysterious way. Second, they accorded a very high status to wandering charismatic leaders, through whom they believed the risen Lord guided the churches by granting special visions and auditions. Third, communities gathered around hosts who extended hospitality to those itinerant charismatics and supported their work. The group's confession, "Jesus is

[4]*Sociology of Early Palestinian Christianity* (Philadelphia: Fortress Press, 1977), pp. 7-8.

Lord", carried with it an awareness of his presence and a
readiness to follow his guidance as relayed through these
prophetic spokesmen.

A cold analysis of this sort has undoubted advantages. It
counteracts our tendency to visualize those first assemblies
as somehow similar to our own congregational life, and it
introduces us immediately into an alien world. Yet at crucial
points this type of analysis fails to help us enter into that
ancient scene. It does not help us to understand the prophet's
message, to validate it, to separate true from false
charismatic gifts, or to join the original audience. As a
method of approach it takes us no closer to understanding
Paul than were the bystanders on Mars' Hill. Although it
makes an understanding of the prophetic gift more urgent, it
does not make it less difficult.

Another method of procedure is to concentrate attention
on the language and the linguistic forms used by the
prophets. It is possible to identify many of these forms. For
one thing, they retain the marks of oral speech, being shaped
by the occasion when prophets addressed congregations of
believers. For another, they reflect the personal experience
of an encounter with the heavenly world, of the overwhelming effect of divine revelation, along with the pressure
exerted by divine threats and promises. This pressure gives
to prophetic discourse a strong hortatory flavor, for the
prophet becomes a spokesman of a God who wants to bring
the behavior of his people under the control of the same
Spirit that animates his prophet. Often this requires from the
prophet an authoritative reinterpretation of Scripture, one
in which the people learn how God now wants them to
discern new meanings in the stories of their past.[5]

A study of linguistic forms corroborates the results of

[5]These marks, with others, have been isolated in Ulrich B. Müller,
Prophetie und Predigt im N.T. (Gütersloh, 1975).

sociological study. The native habitat of prophecy was the gathering of believers for worship, instruction, mutual aid, and guidance on their mission in the world. This gathering formed a highly charged magnetic field in which unusual spiritual powers operated. Those invisible powers made their presence known through diverse visual and auditory signs. Especially manifest in group singing and praying, the signs provided guidance for the congregation as it was drawn more and more into the war being waged between the purposes of God and the stratagems of the devil. In that war the community became vulnerable to confusion, for the demonic world exuded charismatic gifts of its own, designed to deceive the community into adopting less hazardous policies. The shape of warfare thus required that the congregation receive reliable guidance from charismatic leaders, authentic messengers from the true God and the living Christ. Certain gifts equipped some leaders for well-defined and routine tasks (such as teaching). By contrast, the gift of prophecy was much more spontaneous; it stubbornly resisted the process of institutionalization. It was customary for prophets to face emergency situations in which their message was perforce strictly ad hoc. They spoke only when moved by the Spirit, and that impulse was often unanticipated and surprising to both speaker and audience. Of course their work remained no less church-centered than was the work of teachers, inasmuch as each revelation through one prophet called for corroboration from other prophets as well as subsequent acceptance by the congregation as a whole.[6]

The analysis of oral speech forms can be very useful to interpreters. It can underscore the importance of prophecy in the early church and can clarify the basic thrust of such

[6]Cf. Jannes Reiling in Johannes Panagopoulos, ed. *Prophetic Vocation in the N.T. and Today* (Leiden: Brill, 1977), pp. 60-72.

words in the prophet's lexicon as *mystery, revelation, word, sign, repentance, preaching, salvation, prayer, glory, life, beatitudes,* and *woes.* Each of these words has unique connotations that were contributed by its original habitat in the prophet's dialogue with the church.

Yet the study of linguistic forms, even at its best, cannot bridge the distance between charismatic speakers and noncharismatic interpreters. It provides no dependable norms for measuring the validity and the permanent resonance of prophecy. It cannot penetrate the mystery of the invisible source of this gift, whether in God or in the devil, a mystery that is inescapable wherever things divine impinge on things human. It cannot satisfy the prophets themselves by doing justice to their inner experience of the gift, nor does it create effective rapport with the early congregations as they listened for the Spirit to speak in their midst. The distance remains.

I have already said enough to indicate what to me is the greatest single obstacle to be encountered: the elusive distance separating a prophetic speaker from a nonprophetic interpreter. How can an interpreter have enough affinity with the charismatic speaker to comprehend the message? In locating the greatest obstacle at this point we are not far from the original appraisal by the biblical prophets. They recognized that the same Spirit that spoke through the prophet must give listeners the power to interpret the prophet's message. As Paul wrote, "No one comprehends the thoughts of God except the Spirit of God" (1 Cor 2:11). One of the complaints of early Christian prophets was that God's intended audience was subject to a chronic blindness and deafness that only the Spirit could overcome. Those conditions truly baffled the prophets and often brought about the frustration of their mission. If we listen with empathy to their complaint, we must accept their appraisal of the greatest single obstacle to understanding.

The situation is not unlike a journalist's effort to write the story of Mother Teresa.[7] As a nonbeliever, the journalist could not understand or agree with a nun for whom prayer was "the source of her strength and the heart of her achievements." When he asked how she could work so effectively among the poorest of the poor, she answered, "I do nothing; he does it all." He could make no sense of such an answer and was candid enough to admit it.

To return to the main point: according to the prophets themselves, any understanding of their work could take place only where twin gifts of the Spirit converged, the gift of prophecy and the gift of discernment. When we ask if that is still true, and when we measure the answer by current methods of Bible study, it is difficult to know how to answer.

Today the work of interpreting early Christian prophets has been assigned to battalions of professionally trained exegetes (interpreters of texts), to whose work the gift of the Spirit is no longer considered intrinsic. Ancient prophets relied on Spirit-guided interpreters to overcome the distance between God's will and the church's behavior; modern exegetes rely on acceptable academic methods of analysis, which become steadily more elaborate and more esoteric. One contingent of scholars devotes itself to the mastery of complex techniques for winnowing dependable historical data out of traditions that have been shaped by liturgical or pedagogical practices. Another contingent places under the microscope the different types of biblical speech and develops for each type a specialized syllabus of hermeneutical procedures. This current series, and in fact this very volume, illustrates what I have in mind here. I do not deny that this method of study has value, but I want to warn that no such method can by itself overcome the obstacles inherent in the gift of prophecy.

[7]*New York Times Magazine,* Dec. 9, 1979.

On their part, modern evangelists are eager to challenge scholars for their monopoly on exegesis and to substitute a more pragmatic manipulation of Scripture to fit their own recipes for salvation, a procedure which may distort the prophetic message no less seriously. Meanwhile the hills are full of counselors who turn isolated biblical anecdotes into therapeutic advices to ameliorate the private anxieties so endemic in our day. A modern interpreter may claim to be guided by the Holy Spirit, but such a claim invites doubts about whether the Spirit is the same as the one which spoke through John and Paul. We seldom ask what those early prophets might say about our later interpretations. How would they react to scholars who trust in the objectivity of their methods to guarantee an authentic hearing of God's Word? How would they react to preachers who make each prophetic text an instrument for increasing their own fame and income, or who capitalize on faith-healing, or glossolalia, or vast TV audiences, as evidence that they are qualified to speak for Peter or Mark, or, more important, for God?

The point is this: whether exegesis (biblical interpretation) is carried out in the seminar room, in the pulpit, or in a person's living room, it illustrates a major hermeneutical dilemma: how can noncharismatic interpreters do justice to charismatic speakers? It is true that one should not expect among American churches a precise counterpart to the first-century situation in which spiritual gifts were poured out on prophets, on their interpreters, and on their audiences gathered for worship. It would be folly to attempt to duplicate that situation. Yet it may be greater folly to rely on academic dogmatisms, as if one could computerize the movements of the Spirit. Greater folly, also, to use prophetic texts to fuel a revivalist's will to power.

On what terms, then, can the distance between ancient prophets and modern interpreters be reduced? I am convinced that the first step requires that we take more seriously the prophets' own awareness of their roles. They believed that the Spirit had endowed them with an overwhelming power, that God had assigned to them nontransferable and nondeferable tasks, and that it was this assignment that distinguished them from others. If an interpreter finds their work incomprehensible, it may be because that interpreter does not take God's interventions as seriously as did the prophets themselves. Or because an interpreter cannot comprehend how individuals can believe themselves to have been set apart from their community by the very gift that binds them more closely to it. Or because a reader cannot accept the message a prophet asserts has come from God. When we grasp how fully the prophets' work was grounded in their perception of the presence and power of God, we should not be surprised by difficulties in interpretation, nor should we be surprised that only a twin gift from the same Spirit can complete the chain of communication. Because this Spirit, like the wind, blows where it chooses, it will be forever impossible to develop an adequate method for measuring its velocities and consequences. Yet we should not infer that such an origin makes the gift of the Spirit wholly incomprehensible today.

What, then, can be said of the vocation of the prophets? We must be aware of the danger of oversimplification, heeding the thrust of Harris' Law: "Any philosophy that can be put into a nutshell belongs there." Yet there are several recurrent features that cannot be missed. For one thing, the prophets' vocation was often accompanied by visions of the heavenly realm; they perceived realities hidden from other eyes. These visions were often accompanied by a special flow of words that the prophet heard and could not ignore, though they were heard by no one else. These visions and auditions came with such stunning force that recipients were inclined to link them to the epiphanic visitations of God to the patriarchs, to the theophanic experiences of Moses, to the prayers of the Psalmists, or to the moments when God called the great prophets of Israel. Samuel Terrien has placed this whole succession of revealers within the horizons of a single panorama where witnesses became aware of the presence of an absent God and the absence of a present God. As Terrien puts it, "they were the poets of an electing presence," and he cites the words of Henry Wadsworth Longfellow,

> . . . the prophet's vision,
> The exultation, the divine
> Insanity of noble minds.[8]

It would be a mistake, however, to concentrate too much upon the private character of the inner experience. As Jannes Reiling insists, this vocation was from first to last "a church-centered ministry through which the Lord speaks to the church what he wants to say when he wants it said."[9] This message to the church presupposed the covenant that already bound it to its Lord; the message came as a way of renewing, correcting, or fulfilling that covenant. The message normally contained both commands and prohibitions, promises and threats, beatitudes and woes. As we have said, the occasion was provided by a gathering of the church for worship and for listening for divine guidance. The congregation was expected to accord to the prophet the same authority it accorded to the Lord, in whose name both prophet and people discerned their duties and anticipated their destinies. It was God's promises that aroused their deepest hopes, his threats that elicited their strongest fears.

Yet, because God's thoughts and ways were always different from theirs, the message relayed by the prophet usually collided with the group's desires and expectations.

---

[8]*The Elusive Presence* (New York: Harper & Row, 1978), pp. 227.
[9]*Hermas and Early Christian Prophecy* (Leiden: Brill, 1973), p. 13.

The message created an adversary relationship between prophet and people, the prophet being impelled to adopt a position "against the church for the church." Outsiders often joined the prophets in attacks leveled *against* the church, e.g.: "The greatest enemies of religion have always been religious people themselves. The Victorian bishops and clergymen are the real fathers of atheism in England."[10] But only authentic prophets leveled such attacks *for* the church. Accordingly, their interpreters need to share their double motivation: *against* and *for*.

To understand the complexity of this situation, we must recall the continuing tensions between the church and the world at that time. The origin and measure of those tensions is given, once for all, in the crucifixion of Jesus by the political and religious authorities of his day. Loyalty to an executed rebel inevitably alienated the church from those same authorities. Such alienation was inevitably expressed in the ostracism and persecution of the church's prophets, who remained the "vocal" link between that Lord and his people. Such persecution, in turn, qualified these witness/martyrs to serve as guides of the congregations as they responded to external attacks. So vulnerable were the prophets to those attacks that they often faced the prospect of martyrdom in the line of duty. In those days the Cross, far from being a popular bit of jewelry, was a dread symbol for people who might face comparable condemnation. The act of prophesying could only result in aggravating divisions among the churches; those divisions, in turn, could only accentuate the conflict among the various prophets. What was a clear revelation of divine guidance for one prophet could be repudiated by another prophet, especially if that revelation favored a more dangerous line of action.

[10]Gerald Brenan, *Thoughts in a Dry Season* (London: Cambridge University Press, 1978), p. 53.

Inevitably the same conflicts appeared among interpreters of
prophecy. To accept one revelation in preference to another
might well mean the difference between life and death for
interpreters and their congregations. Interpreters must
themselves discern which prophetic word had come from
God and which from the devil.

So the divisions within the church cut through both the
companies of prophets and the companies of interpreters;
such divisions were seen by both prophets and their
interpreters as the earthly manifestations of battles that were
intelligible only against the backdrop of a struggle that had
been going on since Eden. The vocation of prophets included
the discernment of the competing strategies of God and
Satan and the sharing of that discernment with the covenant
people; the vocation of interpreters was to accept a
particular revelation as coming from God and to make it the
basis for action which would determine wealth or poverty,
survival or death.

When one grasps fully the deadly dimensions of this
conflict, one readily sees why the idiom of warfare between
heavenly kingdoms became the vernacular of early Christian
apocalyptic. One can also see why prophets were accorded a
strategic role in the conduct of that warfare, since their
reading of the heavenly scrolls so frequently brought about
their own martyrdom, whether at the hands of family,
Christian brothers, Jewish antagonists, or Roman police
(e.g., 2 Cor 11:23-29). As some writers came to tell the story,
the "noble company of martyrs" reached from the time of
Abel to the time of the final battle, when the devil himself,
along with his chosen weapon, Death, would be banished
(Luke 11:51). The prophets' vocation thus linked them to the
hidden beginnings and the hidden endings of God's creative
work. At the same time, each emergency faced by their
congregations linked them to the same primeval and
eschatological realities. The gift of the Spirit to the prophets

and to their interpreters was designed to make that linkage clear.

Israel had, of course, for centuries interpreted each successive situation in its pilgrimage as an episode in a story that reached back to the beginnings. Because the early Christian prophets continued that practice, their vocation included the task of providing the churches with inspired reinterpretations of Scripture. They discovered that each episode from the past had become perverted by false readings; accordingly their work entailed correcting the false and disclosing the true. Such disclosures provoked bitter conflict with the professional scribes, who relied on their own cautious exegesis of each text. Utilizing a different type of authority, the prophets saw that the Law and the Prophets had been fulfilled in ways repugnant to the scribes; God's actions in the present provided clues to interpretations which forced the prophet to tell each scriptural story in a new way, adapted to a new audience in a new situation. God became a living God, speaking to those children of Abraham who had been raised up out of the stones (Luke 3:8). Accordingly, in becoming the point of contact between God and his people, the prophets became the pivot between the stories of the patriarchs and the crises faced by their own churches. They were free to see new relevance in the ancient stories, and free, as well, to visualize emerging situations in the light of those stories.[11]

To sum up, the vocation of the prophets had many dimensions. They were see-ers and revealers, listeners and broadcasters. Dispatched with a specific message to a specific community, they were assigned to communicate God's will in both speech and action. They served their community as participants in its worship, instructors in its duties, judges

[11]A similar, though more detailed, summary of the prophet's vocation appears in my *I Saw a New Earth* (Washington: Corpus Books, 1968), pp. 97-104, and *To Heal and To Reveal* (New York: Seabury, 1976), pp. 87-91.

and disciplinarians of its actions. They were catalysts of current controversies and reinterpreters of sacred traditions. As one focus of controversy, they were signs and soldiers in the agelong warfare between God and Satan. As links in the chain of God's spokesmen, they represented that whole chain to the degree that the Spirit authorized them to update the message of earlier spokesmen. This vocation began with a call through the Spirit; it was often fulfilled in arrest, trial, conviction, and martyrdom.

David Hill has ventured to compress all these activities within a single sentence: "A Christian prophet is a Christian who functions within the church, occasionally or regularly, as a divinely called and divinely inspired speaker who receives intelligible and authoritative revelations or messages which he is impelled to deliver publicly, in oral or written form, to Christian individuals and/or the Christian community."[12]

There is one feature of this definition which should be noted immediately. In dealing with prophets in the New Testament we are dealing with their work within the context of the churches in their own day. That fact requires us to give a certain priority to questions that are basically historical. To shift attention too quickly to the modern scene would destroy the original chain of communication, from God through the prophet to God's people. Ever and again, it was a crisis within the churches of that day that evoked the disclosure of God's will. We show little respect for the prophet if we ignore that fact. To be sure, the calling of prophets was such as to lead them to update earlier revelations of the will of God. With great freedom they reinterpreted scriptural prophecies to make them bear on current emergencies. They recognized that God's purposes spanned long periods of time in the pilgrimage of his people.

[12]*New Testament Prophecy* (Atlanta: John Knox Press, 1979), pp. 8, 9.

Although they were summoned to declare the presence of God in an urgent situation, they were also made aware of the steadfastness of God from one epoch to another. This feature of their vocation to their own churches has justified later churches in finding perennial relevance in their messages. Priority must be given to historical questions; yet this does not destroy perennial relevance.

Five Guidelines

Having surveyed the scope of the vocation of early Christian prophets, we come back now to the basic hermeneutical question: how can noncharismatic readers do justice to these charismatic messages? What is the minimum rapport that is essential between an ancient author and a modern exegete? I hazard a fivefold answer:

1. An interpreter must believe (believe in the most profound sense) in the God of the prophets as a God who calls and gives specific tasks to specific individuals.

2. An interpreter must belong (and belong in the most profound sense) to a community which has been called into existence and given a distinctive vocation by that same God.

3. An interpreter must be alive (alive in a way open only to participants) to the conflicts which that vocation and those tasks cause—conflicts within the prophets themselves, within the covenant community, and between that community and its neighbors.

4. An interpreter must become highly sensitive to the degree to which these conflicts are the immediate manifestations of a more ultimate warfare between God and hostile heavenly forces.

5. An interpreter must become keenly aware of the invisible threads that link these conflicts to the primal beginnings and final endings of God's purposes for his people and for his creation as a whole.

In the two chapters which follow I will expand this list of guidelines, but I hold these five to be the most basic. Later, as we begin to examine specific texts (chaps. 4-11) we will put these guidelines to the test. Earlier I called attention to the possibility of distinguishing between the larger company of Christian prophets and the smaller group of apocalyptists. Let me now follow up that discussion by observing that for interpreting the work of this latter small group, Guidelines 3, 4, and 5 are especially important. Their vocation involved them deeply in multiple conflicts within their own hearts, within the churches they served, and between those churches and their neighbors. They were called to disclose the hidden roots of those conflicts in the continuing warfare between God and Satan. This entailed uncovering the even more hidden rootage of current dilemmas in primal beginnings (moderns might speak of returning to Square One) and in final endings (moderns often speak of the bottom line). Because this volume deals with the distinctive vocation of these apocalyptic prophets, those three guidelines will be highly relevant. And because it is just those guidelines that seem most alien to our own mentality, we will come back most frequently to them.

2 THE GIFT TO THE CONGREGATION

Among the many charismatic gifts that were active among early Christians, the gift of prophecy was regarded as one of the most important. When the profusion of gifts was creating bedlam in the church in Corinth, Paul urged its members: "Earnestly desire the spiritual gifts, especially that you may prophesy" (1 Cor 14:1). Not all, of course, had received that gift, yet all were enjoined to weigh carefully what their prophets were saying (14:29). As the prophets were "taught by the Spirit," they addressed their messages to those individuals and congregations "who possess the Spirit" (1 Cor 2:13). All who listened to the prophets needed the charismatic gift of discernment (12:10). The two gifts were twins; the birth of one coincided with the birth of the other.

In this chapter, then, we explore that gift which enabled individuals and congregations to comprehend what God was saying to them through their prophets. We take first a story in Luke that illustrates how two different individuals responded to the presence of a prophet; Luke used the two responses as types of responses to the presence of Jesus within the Christian congregations of Luke's own day. The story shows clearly the need for spiritual discernment. It is an account of a dinner to which a religious leader had invited

Jesus (Luke 7:36-50). While the host and his guest were at dinner, a notorious woman broke into the room and did a most controversial thing. She washed Jesus' feet with her tears and shook costly perfume on them. The reactions of the host were instantaneous, though silent, as befitted a good host. "He said to himself, 'If this man were a prophet, he would have known who and what sort of woman this is.'" The implications are clear. A competent prophet would have penetrated the secrets of the woman's heart, and would, on recognizing her sin, have trumpeted God's judgment and demanded repentance. Because Jesus did none of these things, the host concluded that Jesus could not be a prophet. Luke denied those inferences. By telling a parable this guest had reversed the reasoning of his host. He had in fact read the woman's heart and had relayed to her God's forgiveness. At the same time he had read his host's heart, uncovering a sin that had been completely hidden. Jesus' announcement of God's forgiveness of *both* sinners became an implicit invitation to his host to discern the truth about his own heart. But to accept that invitation was too difficult for this host. His self-righteous condemnation of the woman had hidden his own sin from himself. Although the story is set in the time of Jesus, Luke was telling it for the benefit of his own Christian audience, to make clear the character of saving faith (7:50).

Another illustration of the interplay between the prophet's gift and the gift of discernment is found in John's letters to two churches in Asia, the congregations in Smyrna and Laodicea. The risen Christ commanded his prophet to relay his judgment on both of these congregations, and in both cases this judgment reversed their attitudes. In both cases Christ's judgment was so unexpected that it would be accepted only by acute listening to "what the Spirit is saying to the churches." Christ of course knew what had been happening in Smyrna: "I know your tribulation and your poverty . . . I know the slander . . . the devil is about to throw some of you into prison . . ." (Rev 2:8-11; my own translation). But Christ's verdict was this: "You are rich." The situation in Laodicea was quite the reverse (Rev 3:14-19): "You say, 'I am rich, I have prospered and I need nothing.' You do not realize that you are wretched, pitiable, poor, blind, and naked" (my own translation). Through his spokesman, Christ was trying to raise the consciousness of both congregations so that they could grasp his way of calculating security and prosperity. Neither congregation could have understood John without listening with new ears to what the Spirit was saying. That listening would have required the difficult act of imagining how their situation appeared to a Lamb that had been slain.

John's message to the poor in Smyrna and to the rich in Laodicea finds a close parallel in the beatitudes and woes as reported by Luke (6:20-26). In both cases a prophet was addressing a company of disciples. In both he was conveying a total revolution in perspectives that had been accomplished by the revelation of God's judgment in the gift of his kingdom. In both cases a prophet's vision of the invisible was operating in such a way as to correct the common-sense blindness of his listeners. In both cases an immediate blessing and curse were linked to an ultimate judgment.

These samples of prophetic activity are very different from our various modern conceptions of what prophets do. For example, it is commonly supposed that prophets beam their bullhorns at the secular world and demand the immediate reform of a particular economic or governmental institution. When people want to locate a prophet they listen for the most fiery reformer, denouncing the authorities and demanding their abdication or overthrow. And the only gift one needs in order to understand that sort of a prophet is the gift of courage to join the crusade. How different from the situations reflected in Luke 7 and Revelation 2, 3!

Another error is to look for prophets among the most gloomy doomsayers, who set themselves up in conspicuous places and, like scarecrows, frighten passers-by from pursuing their normal occupations. Supreme pessimists, they can foresee nothing ahead but devastation. Because of specific social vices, they pronounce the whole nation guilty, so guilty that God will soon dump on it all the bowls of wrath. No unusual spiritual gift is required to understand such a message.

> He loves to preach an ethic so sublime
> That anything we do becomes a crime.[1]

Still another error is to think of the prophets as wild eccentrics, driven by the obsession for escaping from all the evils of their world. "Their visions of heaven served as security-blankets. All apocalyptic is escapism, pure if not simple." It is true, of course, that the Christ who spoke through early Christian prophets was invisible, "seated at the right hand of God"; also that the movements of the Spirit were as unpredictable and mysterious as the wind. Yet Christ's word, uttered through the prophet, was always spoken to a particular audience at a particular time and place. It always recognized the dilemmas of that audience as the context within which immediate decisions must be made in response to the leading of the Spirit.

The native habitat for the twin charismatic gifts, as made clear by John's letters (Revelation 2, 3), was provided by occasions for worship by Christian congregations. Worship created the magnetic field within which a congregation felt itself to be under the control of the Spirit. It had gathered around a common table where, in eating together, worshipers recalled the whole story of salvation, as that story

[1]Molière, *Tartuffe,* Act 1, Scene 1.

had reached a climax in the Upper Room, in Gethsemane and on Calvary. Worshipers joined in prayers, both spontaneous and formal. These prayers erupted into explosive singing of doxologies and hallelujahs. Leaders invited the Holy Spirit to control all thoughts and words. There was nothing foreign or artificial in this "waiting" on the Spirit, inasmuch as all believers were conscious of having received the Spirit in baptism. Through the Spirit they had died and had been born again as children of the Father, for the coming of whose kingdom they prayed every day. They relied for each day's rations on the grace of that Father. From him they received forgiveness of sins and deliverance from "the Evil One." The Lord's Prayer is an accurate transcript of the basic orientation of congregational experience. One variant in the second petition of that prayer is significant: "May your Holy Spirit come upon us and cleanse us" (my own translation). The presence of that Spirit formed the boundaries of the time and space within which a congregation lived. It was within those boundaries that prophets were summoned to speak and their hearers were summoned to discern what the Spirit was saying.

It is within this habitat that interpreters may most readily comprehend the cluster of convictions that made the ancient prophets' word both intelligible and essential. We must summarize those convictions. First of all was the awareness that all defilement originates in the heart. Nothing that comes from outside a person can contaminate that person; evil comes only from within (Mark 7:1-23). So the state of a person's heart became an ultimate concern; all one's fears and hopes are important clues to that innermost condition.

A second conviction had to do with a person's inability to judge the state of his or her own heart.

As Jeremiah had realized,

> The heart is deceitful above all things,
>   and desperately corrupt;
> who can understand it? (17:9)

Among the sources of deceitfulness was a person's penchant for self-righteousness. Religious leaders were especially prone to self-deception; confidence in their own sincerity simply reinforced the duplicity. Hypocrisy was a term covering a hundred types of self-deception; rarely, if ever, are hypocrites conscious of their own hypocrisy. This fact brought into play a third conviction: only God has perfect knowledge of the heart of an individual or of a congregation.

> For neither man nor angel can discern
> Hypocrisy, the only evil that walks
> Invisible, except to God alone.[2]

And because all hearts are open to God and all desires known to him, his people could be absolutely sure that "nothing is covered up that will not be revealed" (Luke 12:2). All forms of self-deception were seen to be strictly *pro tem*. There would come a time when God's perfect knowledge would be shouted from the housetops. But the prophet did not encourage or tolerate postponement of that future judgment. His work centered in anticipating and announcing that verdict. His assignment was to use the future threat as therapy for healing the blindness of his immediate auditors. Such healing required both speaking

[2]John Milton, *Paradise Lost* (New York: New American Library), iii, 682-83.

and listening in the Spirit during the prayers and songs of a congregation at worship.

This cluster of convictions underlies a Lukan arrangement of several teachings of Jesus (11:53–12:12), teachings designed to prepare the disciples to serve as leaders of the churches after Jesus' death, when they would be needed as his spokesmen. To understand the thrust of the teachings, it is necessary to give full weight to the narrative setting. First of all, Jesus was surrounded by members of his own people who were laying a trap for him in order to find basis for killing him. Second, he was surrounded by "thousands" of his own people who were enthusiastically following him, amazed by his power over the demons and by signs of his prophetic authority. Probably these obverse reactions were related: enthusiasm fueled the hostility, and vice versa. Third, Jesus anticipated a time when these disciples would be placed on trial before synagogues and rulers and authorities (12:11). At this juncture, Jesus began his instruction with a stern warning: "Beware of the yeast of the Pharisees, which is hypocrisy" (12:1; my own translation).

At first glance, this warning seems to express deep animosity toward those who were planning his death. But a closer look shows that Jesus was wholly concerned with a desperate need on the part of his friends. He found hypocrisy to be their own deadliest enemy. In this case their self-deception was hidden by their fears. Because of their allegiance to him, these men would also face death, a prospect that would arouse a powerful fear of "those who kill the body." They were as yet unaware of how powerful that fear could and would become. They could secure a victory over that hypocrisy only by having such a fear of God that all other fears would vanish. Only God, after he has killed, has the power to cast into hell.

The context of these teachings forces an interpreter to deal with all the passions and confusions released by noisy trials

before religious and political judges. The issue was whether
Jesus' spokesmen, when dragged before such trials, would
fear their adversaries or become anxious as to how they
would defend themselves. Their freedom from that fear and
that anxiety would be an index to their freedom from
self-deception. On trial for their lives, their fear of God
would be measured by the strength of their reliance on the
power of the Holy Spirit. Why did Luke place here the saying
about the danger of blaspheming against that Spirit? Perhaps
to define such blasphemy as the sin of a Christian prisoner
who allowed the fear of his prosecutors to displace his trust in
the Holy Spirit. In any case, just as the fear of others signaled
the success of the adversaries, so that gift of fearlessness
marked the decisive defeat of the devil and served as an
effective witness to the power of God. "Don't be afraid. You
are of more value than many sparrows" (12:7; my own
translation).

This discussion should make clear how strategic was the
work of the prophet—and how difficult. Appealing to the
hearts of a Christian audience, he helped them recognize the
presence of a struggle between competing fears. That
struggle was so intense that the temptation to self-deception
was almost overwhelming; the human adversaries were all
too visible and powerful, their master all too invisible and
impotent. The prophet must persuade them to "put eternal
destiny before apparent security and prosperity in the
present."[3] The odds were such as to require the help of the
Holy Spirit before these Christians could "take sides and
choose between earthly and heavenly salvation."[4] As
interpreters, we must take into account this inner struggle
among the prophet's listeners.

[3]J. P. M. Sweet, *Revelation* (Philadelphia: Westminster, 1979), p. 2.
[4]Ibid., p. 10.

The Lukan report can also help interpreters recognize the conjunction of three distinct times that are involved in a prophet's message. First is the time when Jesus' stern warning is issued: Beware of hypocrisy! Then there is the time when the auditors will stand before rulers, on trial for their allegiance to Jesus, a time when the struggle between competing fears will reach its climax. Finally, there is the time of a last accounting in which the Son of man will either acknowledge or deny each of them before the angels of God (12:8, 9). In all three of these times the Son of man would be present, though in different ways; in all three the Holy Spirit would also be present.

The prophet discerns an intimate connection between the trial before human judges (nothing could be more mundane) and the trial before the angels of God (nothing less mundane). In both trials, the secrets of Christian hearts would be revealed. No trace of self-deception could survive those two trials. They would disclose the cosmic truth that corresponds to the state of the heart. So the prophet discerned the hidden connections between fears and hypocrisy on the earthly stage and in the final judgment itself. In his mind, the outer theatre "corresponds to the inner theatre of the beholder,"[5] and the function of the future is to disclose secrets now hidden in the heart or "whispered in private rooms" (12:3). This subtle correlation between present secrets and future judgments is illustrated by a parable in Matthew in which an absent master returns to his house to discover what his stewards have been doing in his absence. He finds that some have been using their privileged position to satisfy their own desires. The penalty sounds strange until the reader recalls the source of their

[5]A. N. Wilder, *Thornton Wilder and His Public* (New York: Fortress, 1980), p. 87.

treachery: these servants are simply classified "with the hypocrites" (Matt 24:51).

Here we may well remember a point made in the preceding chapter, to the effect that it was quite customary for the Christian prophet to trace current dilemmas and decisions of the churches to the invisible warfare between God and Satan. Such a pattern was clearly the case in dealing with the ever-present temptations to self-deception/hypocrisy. As prophets traced the source of all truth to the God of truth, so, too, they traced all deceit to the great deceiver, the devil. He was viewed as the father of lies, the source of inner blindness, the adversary whose chief weapon was his power to deceive the people of God. In this warfare Satan relied upon the accuracy of the proverb: "Deception finds deception." To paraphrase Amos Wilder's axiom: deception in the outer theater finds deception in the inner theater. It is against this background that we can appreciate a double accent in the climactic petition in the Lord's Prayer: "Deliver us from evil." One accent is clarified by the translation: "Deliver us [the followers of Jesus] from the Evil One [the devil, the source of all evil]." The second accent: "Deliver us from his ability to deceive us by playing on our own propensity for deceiving ourselves."

In this regard, the irony in an allegory of C. S. Lewis is quite in line with scripture. One of the major characters is a chief demon named Screwtape. The scene is an annual dinner to celebrate the graduation of a new class from the Tempters' Training College. As part of the celebration Screwtape proposes a toast to the graduating class. First, he praises the wine that has been chosen for this ceremony; it has been blended from several carefully selected strains of hypocrisy. His toast reaches a climax in the words: "It will be an ill day for us if what most humans mean by religion ever vanishes from the earth. . . . Nowhere do we tempt so successfully as on the very steps of the altar."[6]

It is significant that according to all four Gospels, Jesus warned his disciples against hypocrisy; even more significant that according to all four Gospels this warning failed. The disciples all deceived themselves into supposing that they were ready for the coming trial of faith. Jesus had been freed from fear of his adversaries, but they had not. Gethsemane proved that Jesus' early warning against self-deception had been entirely justified. It was not until after his crucifixion that the true state of their own hearts had been disclosed. Then they could better understand the relative weight of the two fears of which Jesus had spoken in Luke 12:4, 5. In his second volume Luke showed the delayed effects of Jesus' martyrdom. On trial before the same court that had convicted Jesus, those fearful disciples had become courageous enough to shout, "We must obey God rather than men" (Acts 5:29). In a very concrete way these friends of Jesus had demonstrated how the fear of God had become the beginning of their wisdom, and how that fear had given them a victory over their earlier self-deception.

This corporate experience on the part of Jesus' disciples should help interpreters understand why prophets so frequently used the Passion story to penetrate the secrets hidden in the hearts of a Christian congregation. In the imagery of the *Revelation to John,* the Lamb that was slain could both discern and disclose the deceptions sponsored by the dragon and his allies. In telling the story of Jesus' death, the words of the prophet became a message from God that had been verified by a victorious Lord. Accordingly, when John saw a mysterious figure in the midst of the seven golden lampstands, he heard that figure say: "I died, and see, I am

[6]C. S. Lewis, *The World's Last Night* (New York: Harcourt, Brace, 1960), pp. 69-70.

alive forevermore; and I have the keys of Death and Hades"
(Rev 1:18; my own translation). When this charismatic word
of the prophet was matched by charismatic listening in the
church in Smyrna, the death of Jesus conveyed power to
overcome the fear of death, which is responsible for the
protean forms of self-deception. Let us listen again to that
letter:

> Here speaks the first and the last, the one who died and
> came to life: "I know your tribulation and your poverty—but
> you are rich! I know the slander of those who say that they are
> Jews and are not, but are a synagogue of Satan. Do not fear
> what you are about to suffer. Beware, the devil is about to
> throw some of you into prison, that you may be tested, and
> for ten days you will have tribulation. Be faithful until death,
> and I will give you the crown of life. If you have an ear, listen
> to what the Spirit is saying to the churches. Whoever
> conquers shall not be hurt by the second death." (Rev 2:8-11;
> my own translation)

This letter from the risen Christ to his church in Smyrna
reflects the pattern of thinking we have been exploring: the
recollection of the Passion story of Christ; the perceptions of
the hidden warfare with the devil; the appeal of Satan to the
fear of death (the first death, of course); the dangers of
self-deception, grounded in false conceptions of what is the
true measure of wealth and poverty; the understanding of
the present emergency as a trial of faith; the realization that
the ultimate "crown of life" will be either lost or won in the
course of that trial; the central concern of the prophet with
the inner resources of this community; his recognition that
only a gift of the Spirit will enable this congregation to listen
to his letter, not as coming from the prophet but as dictated
by the Lord, in whose eyes they are indeed "rich." Now if we
compare this letter to the teaching of Jesus in Luke 12:1-10,
we will notice strong similarities between the prospect of

suffering on the part of the Smyrneans and on the part of Jesus' disciples. We should also notice an equally strong similarity between the two patterns of thinking.

When we assess the work of these two prophets, Jesus and John, we arrive at five more guidelines for interpreting apocalyptic prophecy.

6. An interpreter, in assessing prophetic communication, must have due regard for the dynamics of congregational worship in which the corporate activity of listening for the Spirit proceeds through prayers, hymns, sacramental observance, and through quiet consideration of immediate dilemmas and duties. (This is an extension of Guideline 2, p. 31 above.)

7. An interpreter must recognize the need for the prophet to penetrate the various protective masks of self-deception by which a particular audience is prepared to resist the message and to shunt aside its painful disclosures. (This is an extension of Guideline 3, p. 31 above.)

8. An interpreter must recognize the importance of charismatic listening, the gift of the Spirit to an audience that enables it to see what had hitherto been hidden and by an action of repentance to return to its initial vocation under Christ.

9. Interpreters must be able to trace the subtle correlations between the prophet's announcement of final judgment and the double responses of resistance and repentance. They must be able to recover the linkages between levels of reality that seem to be separate—the psychic, the ethical, the political, the historical, the heavenly and cosmic. (This is an extension of Guidelines 4 and 5, p. 31 above.)

10. Interpreters must become alert to the multiple ways in which the prophet's word and the believers' listening

(e.g., victories over self-deception and fear) represented joint responses to the story of Jesus, as focused
in his death and resurrection. Through those joint
responses, Jesus became mysteriously present to the
worshiping congregation in such a way as to give
immediate force to the narratives and teachings in the
Gospels.

The relevance and efficacy of these guidelines should
become clearer when we examine in greater detail some
specific visions of prophets and some specific experiences of
Christian congregations.

Finally, a word about the function of these guidelines.
They emerge from a double realization: on the one hand,
that it is impossible for modern congregations to duplicate
the charismatic situations in first-century churches; that, on
the other hand, modern interpreters, to have sufficient
rapport with those situations, must fulfill certain specific
qualifications. Thus, as an experiment in analysis, we have
sought to set forth the minimum qualifications that will
enable noncharismatic exegetes to deal fairly with both
partners in that ancient conversation.

We grant that by its very nature such an analysis always
falls short of achieving full empathy. In fact, analysis of a
prophet's message often appears to prevent empathy with
that message. There is nothing entirely new about this
predicament; in one form or another it was present whenever
prophets addressed their own congregations. The prophet
levied certain demands that must be accepted to verify their
status as God's people. Then the prophet could not avoid
asking, "Is this response an authentic mark of repentance
and obedience?" The congregation, on its part, needed to
test the credibility of the prophet, asking, "Is this an
authentic word of the Lord?" Neither question could be
answered without a measure of critical analysis. Otherwise
there would be no true discernment of the spirits. When the

scripture is read in a modern church, the situation need not be wholly different. When in the New Testament lesson, a prophet claims authority over those who listen, the congregation instinctively applies various tests of credibility to the message. The twin gifts are still present, in however attenuated a form. Paul's words are still an apt recognition of this fact: "No one comprehends the thoughts of God except the Spirit of God" (1 Cor 2:11).

3 THE HORIZONS OF APOCALYPTIC PROPHECY

In the first two chapters, we have explored the sense of vocation among early Christian prophets and among early Christian congregations. We called attention to the conjunction of those vocations as gifts of the Holy Spirit. We observed that both prophets and congregations were absorbed in securing guidance for the present moment, and that in this sense both vocations were stubbornly this-worldly rather than escapist in character; they were concerned with God's will at a particular place and a particular time. Normally that will was discerned most clearly and most disturbingly in the story of Jesus' humiliation and glorification. When listened to as an expression of God's will, that story issued its own summons to share in his humiliation and glorification. In this way the gospel created a firm linkage between Jesus' story and their own, so that the axis between crucifixions became the base line for the interpretation of prophecy (e.g., Gal 6:14).

Beginning from that base line, we need to explore an aspect of those vocations which seems to contradict any concern with the present moment: the visions of the end. These visions appear to identify the end of Christian vocation with the end of history, a realm wholly beyond

human experience. This concern for the end of time gives to
New Testament prophecy an apocalyptic extremism that
renders it either unintelligible or unacceptable to many in the
twentieth century.

For many scholars, the announcement of an impending
end of time is a sole and sufficient definition of apocalyptic
thought, a definition that makes apocalyptic thought wholly
different from prophetic. For them, prophecy concentrates
on the historical realm, whereas apocalyptic deals with a
realm beyond history. The former is basically optimistic with
regard to God's power to redeem the time; the latter is
totally pessimistic. The former anticipates changes within
the present structures of society; the latter anticipates
unimaginable cosmic cataclysm. The former confers on
people the power to shape their own future; the latter is
wholly fatalistic. I am not satisfied with such a definition of
apocalyptic, and I shall seek in the following pages to show
why.

As an example of an apocalyptic expectation of world's
end consider Matthew 24, a text in which Jesus' disciples
asked him privately concerning the close of the age and in
which Jesus made several dramatic predictions. The coming
of the Son of man would be like the days when Noah entered
the ark. Heaven and earth would pass away. In fact Jesus
said that before that very generation passed away, people
must expect things like the following:

the sun will be darkened,
and the moon will not give its light,
and the stars will fall from heaven,
and the powers of the heavens will be shaken; . . .
all the tribes of the earth will mourn, . . .
they will see the Son of man coming on the clouds
    of heaven with power and great glory; . . .
he will send out his angels with a loud trumpet call,

and they will gather his elect from the four winds,
    from one end of heaven to the other (vv 29-31).

Such expectations were by no means foreign either to
Jesus or to early Christian prophecy (Mark 13; Luke
17:22-37; 21:10-36; 1 Thess 4, 5; Heb 12:18-29; 1 Peter 4; Rev
6-9; 18-20). Scholars label these expectations as pure
apocalyptic, since they anticipated sudden, total cosmic
catastrophe. What seems to be pictured was nothing less
than the end of our universe, the cessation of time, the
termination of history in oblivion. After such a climax to the
human story it would seem that nothing more could
transpire. To be sure, the Gospel spoke of survivors, but
modern readers find survival quite unthinkable after such a
solar disaster. Few predictions have ever been made with
such melodramatic force. The massive walls of the temple
would crumble, while the spoken words of a martyred
prophet would survive the passing away of heaven and earth.
Jesus' followers would be put to death—but they would
nevertheless be saved. Their mission to all nations would
succeed—but through what appeared to be total failure.
False messiahs would show greater wonders than the true, in
order to mislead the elect; yet the true Messiah would
overcome that deception. Nothing that had happened since
the beginning of creation could compare with events that
were announced as soon to happen.

Who was speaking? Jesus, the prophet. Where? The
Mount of Olives, long regarded as the place of messianic
disclosure and fulfillment. When? Two days before the most
strategic Passover in human history, which would be marked
by Jesus' final struggle with adversaries, both human and
demonic, and by his condemnation and execution. To whom
was he speaking? To his disciples. Why? Jesus wanted to
prepare them for work that would involve their own
martyrdom. He wanted to disclose the cosmic repercussions

of their mission, to reinforce their own endurance, confidence, watchfulness, and faithfulness.

What are we to make of such a prospect? Let me begin with three observations. (1) Because the vision represented the consummation of the purposes of the God who had called the prophet, the vision must convincingly express the power and the goodness of that God. A succinct statement of this principle is Paul's assurance: "He who calls you is faithful, and he will do it" (1 Thess 5:24). (2) Because the calling had drawn its recipients into deadly conflicts with antagonistic forces in religion, politics, and culture, the vision must deal with both the accentuation and the resolution of those conflicts, by picturing the final verdict on God's enemies and the vindication of God's servants. Because the salvation of executed criminals appeared to be quite impossible in human terms, the vision of the end must seem to be equally impossible . . . in human terms. (3) Because the same vocation had been given by the Messiah to his prophetic spokesmen, to their interpreters, and to the messianic community as a whole, the vision of the end must respect this solidarity in mission by including them all in the same consummation. "He will gather his elect . . . "

It is one thing to analyze the logic behind such a vision and quite another thing to convince readers of its "truth." For most modern readers a quite different logic becomes applicable. Such announcements of the end of the world, having been disproved by events themselves, force us to reject a speaker's authority and knowledge. Thus something further is needed if we are to defend the sanity of these early prophets.

We begin such a defense by observing that Jesus and his followers were not the first to prophesy in terms of darkened suns and bloody moons. They were using a vocabulary, a set of linguistic idioms, that was entirely conventional. Those linguistic habits had already emerged during the pre-

Christian period, to express God's ways of dealing with his people and with his whole creation. Consider a few samples of this vocabulary:

The writer of Job, representative of a wide range of wisdom literature, stressed the conviction that it is God

> who removes mountains, and they know it not,
> when he overturns them in his anger;
> who shakes the earth out of its place,
> and its pillars tremble;
> who commands the sun, and it does not rise;
>   who seals up the stars; . . . (9:5-7)

From the prophetic predecessors of Jesus, consider Joel and Isaiah.

> The earth quakes before them,
>   the heavens tremble.
> The sun and the moon are darkened,
>   and the stars withdraw their shining.
>
>   (Joel 2:10)

> I will give portents in the heavens and on the earth, blood and fire and columns of smoke. The sun shall be turned to darkness, and the moon to blood, before the great and terrible day of the Lord comes.
>
>   (Joel 2:30, 31)

> For the stars of the heavens and their constellations
>   will not give their light;
> the sun will be dark at its rising
>   and the moon will not shed its light.
>
>   (Isa 13:10; cf. 60:2, 19)

As one recalls Old Testament passages like these, one is forced to conclude that every essential feature in the New Testament prophecies was an echo of these. No Christian prophet tried to explain the meaning of these references to solar disasters, a fact that suggests that the audience was expected to understand the language. The vocabulary was fully indigenous to the community in which the prophet functioned. Modern readers, therefore, must compare this idiom not with modern views of the cosmos but with an ancient outlook within which an intelligible message was conveyed without undue difficulty.[1]

As we study that ancient outlook we find six recurrent convictions which together provide the context for these predictions of solar catastrophes.

(1) Basic to all others was the conviction that the God of Israel had created the sun, moon, stars, and everything else in heaven and on earth. Because he had first established the orbits of the luminaries, his own purposes in creation were responsible for the regular succession of days, weeks, months, and years. They declared his glory. Perhaps it is the erosion of this conviction that, more than anything else, has made obsolete for us the poetic imagery which was the vernacular of prophetic vision.

(2) As creator, God had retained full power over the movements of the heavenly bodies. This means that whenever he chose he could seal up the stars and command the sun not to rise (Job 9:7). Thus both the regularity of the seasons and their interruption alike attested his governance of all things. All visible bodies were manifestations of his invisible design.

(3) For God's people to worship the solar bodies became a prime form of idolatry, since they thereby substituted the worship of creature for adoration of the creator. This idolatry sought to exploit for partisan purposes those gifts which God had intended to benefit all peoples. In the

[1] I have analyzed in greater detail this reliance of the New Testament writers on the Old Testament in an essay, "Some Archetypal Origins of Apocalyptic Predictions," *Horizons in Biblical Theology* 1 (1979):105-36.

development of apocalyptic thought, reverence for the dependability of the zodiac came to be correlated with the worship of other invisible heavenly powers, demonic lords like Mars, Mammon, or Caesar.

(4) God used light and darkness as a means of disciplining his own people. Isaiah's couplet disclosed the basic correlation:

> I form light and create darkness,
>   I make weal and create woe   (45:7)

Since the sun's light was a prime symbol of "weal," i.e., welfare and security in God's presence, the darkening of the sun represented "woe," i.e., insecurity and alienation from God. So Ezekiel saw darkness fall on Pharaoh (32:7); Amos beheld the sun going down at noon on Israel (8:9); Jeremiah saw an eclipse on Jerusalem (15:8, 9); Micah saw the day becoming black over the false prophets (3:6). A darkened sun was used as shorthand for the punishment of peoples who resisted God. His no *is* darkness.

(5) God always remained accessible as an alternate source of light. He could himself be called a sun (Ps 84:11), a sun that rises in the very darkness of the solar system. In his light human beings could see light. The judgment on evil (representing the collusion of demonic and human adversaries) took the form of falling stars; conversely the same idiom reflected God's decision to deliver the elect.

(6) This whole cluster of convictions was grounded in and reflected the Genesis story, in which there is a clear distinction between the creation of two types of light and two corresponding types of darkness. The solar bodies were formed on the *fourth* day of creation; they served to separate one type of light from the type of darkness parallel to it. But another type of light altogether appeared on the *first* day, when God had commanded, "Let there be light." This light

and the darkness appropriate to it were prior to, and therefore superior to, what was created on the fourth day. Prophetic utterance preserved this basic contrast. Warnings of cosmic destruction were congruent to God's action on the *fourth* day; by contrast, the promises of the day of the Lord gave priority to the primal light of the *first* day, when the entire story had begun, and when God had disclosed the primal power of his sovereign mercy.

This appeal to the first day, before sun and moon had been created, is not unlike e. e. cummings' ode to love:

> love is the voice under all silences,
> the hope which has no opposite in fear;
> the strength so strong mere force is feebleness:
> the truth more first than sun more last than star.[2]

The more we penetrate into these linguistic conventions of the Old Testament, the more readily we should be able to grasp the message of Matthew 24. The grammar of images preserves the interdependence of protology and eschatology: this interdependence is necessary if the *fulfillment* of vocation under God is faithfully to represent the *origin* of that vocation. The linguistic habits of the prophets may become clearer if we study how fully each feature in the story of the first day had become imbedded in early Christian anticipations of the last day, when, they believed, the victory of Christ would vindicate the transcendent glory of God.

"In the beginning God created the heavens and the earth . . . . " That action of God constituted the deepest conviction and therefore the furthest horizon of biblical thought. Accordingly, the anticipation of a coming earthquake and heaven-quake brought the present moment within the range of a renewal of God's creative activity.

[2] e. e. cummings, *95 Poems* (New York: Harcourt, Brace, 1958), from poem #94.

"Darkness was upon the face of the deep . . . . " Jewish exegesis before the New Testament period had interpreted this text in terms of a primeval conflict between God and Tiamat or Leviathan; memory of this tradition prompted prophets to find in that struggle the paradigm for contemporary victories over all the abysmal forces of evil.

"The Spirit of God was moving over the face of the waters." Early Christian perceptions of the Holy Spirit can be understood only as echoes of this story. The new creation—whether of the individual, the community, or the whole universe—represented the work of this same Spirit. Active in the resurrection of Jesus and in the rebirth of each believer, this primeval Spirit was the source of all the gifts and signs that punctuated the course of eucharistic worship. Every new victory over the evil powers became a reminder of the initial victory of the Spirit over "the waters" and therefore a token of the firstfruits of the coming harvest.

"And God said . . . " New Testament thinkers were unanimous in recognizing the primal authority and power of God's word. This word was "in the beginning . . . with God." It "dwelt among us, full of grace and truth" . . . it is "the good news which was preached" . . . believers became new beings when they received "with meekness the implanted word" . . . "Filled with the Holy Spirit [disciples] spoke the word of God with boldness" . . . "and the word of God increased . . . . " When one considers all the cognate idioms—hearing, speaking, obeying, deafness, the trumpets and the thunders of judgment—the vision of solar bodies quaking before this voice becomes entirely transparent.

"Let there be light . . . . " A full exposition of this motif would embrace New Testament theology as a whole. The victory of this light over the darkness that rebelled against it was the spur to much eschatological reflection. Because the Day of the Lord is linked to this word of God, sons of the Day were not overcome by darkness. Their blindness had been healed by "the light of the world," clear evidence of the Messiah's authority and reminder of his earlier presence with God in the beginning. Within this cluster of attitudes, to speak of walking in the light was more than a description of daily behavior; it grounded that behavior in a divine realm that transcends the rise and fall of empires. As the prophet John said, those who walk in this light need no sun or moon, for their light is the Lamb.

"Let us make man in our image . . . . " This idea of the image of God was the focus of much early Christian thinking about the two creations, old and new. As those Christians tried to describe the wonder of the new age, they had frequent recourse to earlier ideas of the image of God, ideas which often were expressed by the term *glory*. The glory of God had shone in the face of Jesus Christ. The followers of Christ were being changed into the likeness of Christ "from one degree of glory to another," and ultimately all creation would obtain "the glorious liberty of the children of God." The coming of the Messiah with this primeval glory became the basis for confidence in the return of the Son of man "in the glory of his Father." This whole pattern of thought lay behind the reference to the darkening of the sun at the crucifixion of Jesus (Mark 15:33). Those who, like Jesus, endured martyrdom would by their deaths testify to both the darkness of the world and the dawn of a new day.

God "breathed into his nostrils the breath of life; . . . man became a living being." All versions of Christian eschatology centered in the gift of life. The myth of origins takes many forms: the tree, the garden, the river, the book; but all forms sought to convey this mystery and miracle—the renewal of God's gift of life in the creation of a second Adam. Because this miracle pointed backward to the period before the entrance of sin and death, it also pointed forward to a final victory over those aboriginal enemies.

In a Jewish apocalypse, written near the New Testament

period, we find similar conjunctions between visions of the
end and the Genesis traditions of the beginnings.

> For you Paradise is opened, the tree of life is planted;
> The future age made ready, blessedness prepared;
> The city built, a resting place appointed;
> Good works created, wisdom prepared . . .
> Death hidden, Hades put to flight,
> Corruption forgotten, sorrow passed away . . .
>   (4 Esdras 8:52-53; translated by W. Schmithals)

When we approach Matthew's predictions of a darkened
sun from the standpoint of a modern cosmology, such
predictions appear to be either meaningless or mistaken. But
when we recover the linguistic habits of early prophets, we
can discern the brutal facts of their faith. Prophets trusted in
the connections they discerned between their own struggle
with evil and the purposes of God in the beginning.
Accordingly, the literary accounts of their visions come to us
not as the childish fancies of a prescientific age, but as the
basic patterns of thought by which adults who had come to
share the vocation of Jesus came to terms with the beginning
and the end of God's own work.

In this respect some Christian poets are legitimate
successors of the ancient prophets in discerning the force of
those paradigms. Consider the lines of this hymn:

> The heaven that hides him from our sight
>   Knows neither near nor far:
> An altar candle sheds its light
>   As surely as a star;
> And where the loving people meet
>   To share the gift divine,
> There stands Christ with unhurrying feet;
>   There heavenly splendors shine.
>   (Howard Chandler Robbins)

Artists also can grasp the language that speaks of falling stars and bloody moon. In many of Dürer's illustrations of the Apocalypse, bizarre pictures of heavenly warfare are placed immediately above idyllic pictures of an undisturbed German countryside. The artist penetrates beneath the quiet, complacent surface of ordered living and uncovers subterranean conflicts within both souls and society. He projects these conflicts onto a screen of cosmic warfare. The fact that such warfare is invisible to sleeping villagers may demonstrate rather than disprove its actuality. At any rate, the apocalyptic prophet, like Dürer, was concerned with this juncture of inner conflicts and external though unseen forces.

Even so, the language of cosmic upheavals will remain for many of us a foreign tongue which we will never be able to use with fluency and integrity. We will prefer other biblical analogies, no less dramatic in force, to express confidence in a future completion of whatever work God has begun. Let me mention a few:

Item: In Matthew 24 we find an alternative image in the parable of the man who leaves his home in the care of slaves, each with an assigned task, and with doorkeepers as watchmen awaiting his return. If he comes in the night, will he find them at their posts? This parable provides a graphic picture of the beginning and end of each steward's vocation (vv 45-51).

Item: The figurative appeal to names in the book of life. As a prophet, John tells his readers that they have names that have been written in the book of life from the foundation of the world. If they remain faithful they will receive on their foreheads "the name of the city of my God" (Rev 13:8; 3:5, 12).

Item: The idea of the Sabbath Rest. As the preacher in the Epistle to the Hebrews is interpreting Scripture, including the Genesis account of the Seventh Day, he tells his congregation that when they meet the demands of "Today," they enter the Rest which has been finished from the foundation of the world and they also anticipate a coming celebration of that same Sabbath Day (Heb 4:1-5).

Item: The announcement of the kingdom of God with its call to repent. Like the Sabbath Rest, this kingdom has been prepared from the foundation of the world, and is now established in the heavens. Announcement of its coming to earth precipitates conflict with the powers of evil. By accepting that conflict and by seeking first God's kingdom, his children become heirs of that realm; that promise of inheritance spans both their entire past and their entire future.

Item: The Johannine thought-pattern that stresses the spatial metaphors of whence, where, whither. All who are born of God and share the mission of the Son have the same origin and their work is oriented toward the same destination. Ultimately they are united in the same *where*: "Where I am, there will you be also."

In short, the horizons of prophetic vision were not dependent on a single cluster of images. No single metaphorical pattern displaced all others. In the case of each pattern, the linguistic origins can be traced back to the Old Testament archetypes and to the continuing experience of the synagogue. The origins must be traced also to imaginations that have been activated by the experience of conversion and by life within "the body of Christ."

In the kaleidoscope of images that evoke the unseen horizons of existence, one common factor is to be noted. In them all, prophets receive God's gift of perception and seek to communicate that gift to their audiences.

    ● Discerning signs has to do . . . with perceiving the saga of salvation within the era of the Fall. It has to do with the ability to interpret ordinary events in both apocalyptic and eschatological connotations, to see portents of death where others find progress or success but, simultaneously, to behold tokens of the reality of the resurrection or hope where others are consigned to confusion or despair.[3]

Another factor is common to these metaphors that deal with the horizons of prophetic vision. They all rely upon a common stock of archetypes that over the centuries have permeated the imagination of Israel, and, as Amos Wilder has insisted, "The imagination forfeits due nourishment when the archetypes are silenced."[4]

Five More Guidelines

We now summarize the discussion of this chapter by adding five more Guidelines for the interpretation of apocalyptic prophecy, with special reference to predictions of the end of the world.

11. An interpreter must analyze the language of such predictions by reference to the lexicon of metaphors and images provided by the Old Testament.

12. To the maximum degree possible, an interpreter's imagination must become congenial to the figurative, poetic, parabolic, and mythic character of the prophets' messages.[5]

13. An interpreter must show due regard for the ways in which biblical thinking about the end was shaped to correspond to thinking about the beginning of God's creation.

14. An interpreter must avoid various anachronisms that

[3]William Stringfellow, *An Ethic for Christians and Other Aliens in a Strange Land* (Waco: Word Books, 1973), p. 138.

[4]*Thornton Wilder and His Public* (Philadelphia: Fortress, 1980), p. 55.

[5]For sample interpretations of such apocalyptic symbols as the clouds and the trumpets, see my book *Christian Hope and the Second Coming* (Philadelphia: Westminster, 1954).

stem from measuring prophetic visions of the end by modern measurements of time, e.g.,

—by pegging the end event as predicted by the prophet at any date on a particular human calendar,

—by assuming that such a vision can be validated or invalidated by empirical observation of events on the historical plane,

—by assuming that an objective observer can measure by calendar years the distance from the date of the prophet's message to the fulfillment (or nonfulfillment) of his vision.

15. Realizing that future expectations are ways of reflecting upon present experience, an interpreter must relate specific prophetic visions of coming events to that present by way of dealing with the whence and whither of such communal experiences as:

—faithfulness to Christ and its vindication
—betrayal of Christ and its penalties
—blindness to Christ's power and its cure
—consciousness of sin and its forgiveness
—the memory and the hope bestowed by the sacraments
—self-deception and the gift of self-knowledge

When such guidelines are not followed, a syndrome of attitudes begins to operate, attitudes that virtually guarantee faulty interpretations. (1) An exegete reduces to human predictions what the prophet has heard as divine promises. (2) The predictions are separated from their source in the charismatic vocation of the prophet and the congregation. (3) The interpreter assumes that the accuracy of the predictions provides a dependable index of the prophet's credibility. (4) Later historical developments are seen to prove the predictions false. (5) This proof is taken as evidence of the superiority of the position of the exegete and of the vindication of modern methods of dealing with Scripture. (6) The interpreters and the readers are absolved of any obligation to take seriously the prophetic message of a final judgment.

PROPHETIC VISIONS
AND
CONGREGATIONAL DISCERNMENT

4 A VISION OF HEAVEN
(Revelation 4:1–8:1)

New Testament apocalyptic was the literary product of what the early church understood as the activity of the Holy Spirit. We have now seen that this activity took a double form, embracing both the message of the prophet and the response of the congregation. Together, the message and the response were instrumental in defining the vocation of God's people, giving to that vocation a beginning and an end in the hidden purposes of God. By examining the various dimensions of that vocation we have pointed out fifteen guidelines that may be of help in the work of interpretation. We now turn toward a more sustained analysis of four prophetic visions and four typical aspects of congregational experience which reflect this charismatic setting. We hope that such an analysis will demonstrate the relevance of the guidelines for understanding still other texts in the New Testament.

We begin this second stage of our study with the vision of the prophet John as recorded in Revelation 4:1-8:1. We urge readers to keep this text open for frequent checking.

In approaching this text we have found Amos Wilder's epigraph highly relevant: "Before the message there must be the vision, before the sermon, the hymn, before the prose, the poem."[1]

The vision. In Revelation 4 the message *is* the vision. On the invitation of an angel the seer enters heaven through an open door and sees the thrones there. Nothing happens outside the context of this vision. Every interpreter must adjust his eyes to this heavenly stage with its lighting, its noises, its cast of characters.

The hymn. This heavenly music is not extrinsic to the action, for the words of the chants carry the central thrust of the vision. As in all the best anthems, these choirs address their songs to God (4:8, 11) and to the Lamb (5:9, 12, 13). Sooner or later, all the actors on the stage become singers in these choirs.

The poem. The very climax of the vision takes the form of an extended bit of poetry (7:15-17). This poetic symbol seeks to express the paradox by which a Lamb that was slain had become the shepherd and the refuge for his followers who have washed their robes white in his blood. (The intentional mixing of metaphors is part of the poetic technique.) This poem linked the worship of God in heaven to that worship on earth that had been accomplished by saints who remained faithful through great tribulation.

The very form of John's message thus requires of every reader a special sensitivity to the kind of truth that can be conveyed by visions, hymns and poems.

● Every author has a right to expect from his readers a respect for his units of thought. Just as a preacher resents the custom of journalists who quote only the most provocative sentence from a sermon, so John would resent exegetes who ignore the unity and integrity of a particular vision. He knew nothing about later divisions into chapters and verses; he

[1]*Theopoetic* (New York: Harper & Row, 1977), p. 1.

adopted an architectural design that was far more spacious. This particular vision covers no fewer than four chapters. No scene within those chapters can retain its full force if it is disjoined from the entire sequence.

In the opening scene (chap. 4) the prophet is introduced into the control center of all reality, to the throne room of God in heaven. He responds positively to the command of an angel and to the gift of the Spirit. He is overwhelmed by the ineffable radiance and glory that surround the throne. Showing appropriate hesitation about describing God himself, the prophet affirms that the occupant of this throne lives forever and that all creation praises him day and night. All lesser thrones and sovereignties "cast their crowns" before this king over all kings, giving unceasing witness to their total dependence on and indebtedness to him. As majestic adoration circles around the central throne, so, too, do fearful potencies move out from the same invisible point. One wonders whether any vision of God's throne could be more awesome, more colorful, more mysterious. (Has any Byzantine mosaic or Belgian painter done greater justice to the grandeur of this subject?)

In dealing with any literary art form of this sort interpreters are obliged to adopt the perspective of the artist before venturing their own independent reactions. They are also obliged to avoid premature translation of a vision into prosaic concepts. Having said that, however, I think it safe to say that this vision discloses three features in the prophet's perspective. First of all, the vision is John's way of expressing the truth of the first commandment: "I am the Lord your God. . . . You shall have no other gods before me" (Exod 20:2, 3). The vision constituted one man's answer to the question, What does it mean to confess faith in God?

In the second place, the vision makes clear John's realization that faith in God was far more than verbal assent to formal doctrine. His perception of the heavenly worship of the elders and the living creatures was a way of viewing the "other side" of the empirical existence of the seven churches in Asia. The radiance of the thrones in heaven, the reverberation of thunder from those thrones, provided the true context for the doxologies that were being sung in Smyrna and Laodicea.

In the third place, the vision described the place of origin of the shared vocation that bound the prophet to the churches. It conveyed a sense of the highest source of authority underlying their shared mission. It answered the question why they should accord priority to that mission, a priority far higher than the need for wealth or health or public approval. Every effort to fulfill that vocation could be viewed as a way by which churches joined in singing the heavenly hymns.

> ● In terms of defining the source of vocation of prophet and people, Revelation 4 fulfilled a function not unlike the function Søren Kierkegaard referred to in his personal papers. This 19th century Dane testified that every morning before he could begin any other task he was impelled to satisfy his own mind with fresh confidence in the existence of God. Cf. *Point of View for My Work as an Author.* [2]

But the more we appreciate the splendor of this vision in chap. 4, the more important it becomes to ask what was deficient in it. The best clue to an answer lies in the substance of chap. 5, inasmuch as the prophet seeks there to supply what was still missing. He does this by describing the symbol of the scroll with seven seals, and the anguish of the prophet because no one had been found worthy to open those seals. Although we must again beware of too facile a translation of visual symbol into conceptual prose, we hazard a suggestion.

[2]Trans. Walter Lowrie (New York: Oxford University Press, 1939), p. 66.

Worship of "the one who sits upon the throne" (full obedience to the first commandment) does not in itself solve the manifold riddles of existence. The praise of God may in fact intensify human inabilities to discern his control of earthly events. Can God's glory be truly celebrated apart from a discernment of his ways of being present within the context of human histories? How authentic are the doxologies of chap. 4 when we consider contrary evidence: the infinite tragedies built into human stories, including the affluence of the cruelest and the agonies of the gentlest?

> If God is God He is not good,
> If God is good He is not God;
> Take the even, take the odd,
> I would not sleep here if I could
> Except for the little green leaves in the wood
> And the wind on the water.[3]

Is the vision of chap. 4 credible? Only when the vision of chap. 5 is added to it. That, at least, seems to be the answer of John himself. His vision of the opening of the scroll has the effect of focusing all attention upon the significance of one event in human history—the slaughter of the Lamb. By that act the Lamb had ransomed for God a whole kingdom of saints. He had secured for them the power to rule the earth. He had enabled the whole creation to join in a new song before God's throne. In fact, the throne of God and the throne of the Lamb had become one throne (an impossibility if one insists on literal sense). Therefore the adoration of the elders and the prayers of the saints, fused into a single anthem, had become an anthem of the most paradoxical sort—all power and wealth and wisdom and glory and beatitude are now defined by the slaughter of that Lamb.

[3]Archibald MacLeish, *JB* (Boston: Houghton Mifflin, 1961), p. 11.

It is therefore quite clear that this feature in the vision (Revelation 5) gives an answer to the question of what it meant for John to confess faith in Jesus Christ. His vision is an articulation in light and sound of the second article in the later creed. It releases inaudible reverberations from an event that marked the fusion in human history of glorification and humiliation. It traces the origins and the cohesions of the universal community to what the Lamb had accomplished by that act of ransom. By doing this, the vision suggests how every word in the heavenly doxologies must be redefined by the opening of the seals. Angelic worship is forever bound to a specific time and place in the human story; the "other world" of the throne is made inseparable from the "this world" of the Cross.

● The interpreter must become highly aware of this fusion of perspectives, for it is native to all Christian apocalyptic. This comment may be made clearer by putting next to each other the following two statements. The first is from Martin Buber, explaining why he cannot accept Jesus as Messiah: "Either one takes the condition of the world seriously or one does not. If one does, then its transformation has clearly not occurred and the Christian claim to have found in Jesus of Nazareth the Messiah of God cannot be honored." The second statement is from Paul W. Meyer: "Only Christians have a Good Friday. Only they recall in text and liturgy a public historical event that once made, and still makes, a mockery of their most central claim, and yet (they) return to it as their most central truth: the coming of the Messiah in an unredeemed world."[4]

We must now point out that just as the vision of chap. 4 is incomplete without the extension of that vision in chap. 5, so too the combined visions of those two chapters require a new

[4]*Princeton Theological Journal,* 2 (1979): 223-24.

extension into chap. 6. The seals of the scroll have not yet been opened by the Lamb. The Lamb's worthiness to open those seals has been vindicated, but the impact of that action on the story of humanity has not yet been described. Presumably there is still something lacking both in the heavenly worship and in the earthly experience that is celebrated in that worship. Where may we now locate that deficiency? Surely in the symbolic action involved when the Lamb breaks the seven seals, one after another.

We look especially at the scene revealed when the Lamb opened the fifth seal. The prophet saw under the heavenly altar many souls, people who had been martyred because of their loyalty to God's word and their devotion to his assignment. These people had joined in the worship (chap. 4) and in the confession of Jesus' victory (chap. 5). The triumph of the Lamb had been disclosed to them. But his power to ransom people for God (5:9) had not produced any significant change in the tragic character of human life. It had, in fact, simply initiated a process in which those people most faithful to him had been killed! They had indeed presented their bodies as living sacrifices before God's altar. But in what sense could they be said to share in the Lamb's victory? That became *the* central question.

● Nothing qualifies an interpreter to comprehend this vision so rapidly or so fully as public hostility and imprisonment, incurred because of faithfulness to the Christian way. Many prisoners have discovered in their prison the uncanny relevance of the book of Revelation to both internal and external struggles. Samples of this are diaries and letters written in prison by Christian leaders during World War II: Martin Niemoeller, Hanns Lilje, Roland dePury, Ernst Wiechert, et al. Such witnesses have earned the right to unveil the deeper meanings of John's visions to the rest of us.

It could not be said that their fate had been accidental. Their deaths had illustrated, at least in part, the terrible riding of the four horsemen: the sword, famine, pestilence, wild beasts of the earth. These martyrs would not have suffered if they had not served their sovereign Lord. What price their loyalty? What vindication could they expect? And when?

The opening of the sixth seal disclosed the fate of their enemies—the kings, magnates, generals, millionaires. How did the victory of the Lamb produce any kind of justice for them? And when would such retribution overtake them? Did the Lamb actually exercise sovereignty over them? In John's day, faith in the Cross would have become void had it not provided some sort of answer to such continuing brutalities and injustices.

Accordingly, we see the opening of the seals as giving an answer to the question of what it means to confess faith in Christ's promise to the martyrs. (E.g., "I have not come to bring peace, but a sword"; "whoever loses his life for my sake . . ." "Blessed are you when men revile you and persecute you.") It means that followers of Jesus remain witnesses to his sovereign power even in an "unredeemed world." It means to believe that behind the affluence and power of the "kings of the earth" there is a quiet despair and frustration (the sixth seal). It means that by their very weakness the martyrs give an authentic witness to the power of the Lamb. It means that the ultimate choice facing John's first readers was either to dwell under the altar or to beg the mountains to hide them from "the face of him who is seated on the throne."

> ● We have already discussed the angle from which the predictions of solar darkness can be understood—above pp. 51 ff. So, too, it is clear that John's use of the four horsemen must be understood against the background of Scripture. He

did not have in mind future catastrophes, but rather the
continuing role of Death and Hades in their apparent threat
to everything human. Cf. below chaps. 8, 9.

It should be obvious to every reader that John's vision
would have been incomplete if it had ended at 6:17.
Confidence in the victory of the Lamb and of his martyrs
required a vision of their ultimate reunion. We find that
vision in chap. 7, which therefore becomes a genuine climax
to this visit to heaven. Here the prophet penetrates to the
"other side" of the deaths of the martyrs. Here the prayers
embodied in their total self-sacrifice (6:10) are answered in at
least three ways.

(1) John hears from an angel that 144,000 slaves of God
have received on their foreheads the seal of God. This
number represents God's blessing on each of the twelve
tribes of Israel. His covenant with his ancestral people is thus
fulfilled. (No number could more fully represent perfection
than 12 x 12 x 1,000.)

(2) John's vision, which began in chap. 4 with the throne
of God surrounded by the elders, now expands to include an
immeasurable choir of worshipers drawn from all national,
linguistic, racial, and religious communities. Their white
robes symbolize a purity of self-sacrifice and a totality of
devotion to the God of gods (vv 9-12).

(3) At the end comes a poetic coda—these martyrs
receive as shepherd the martyred Lamb. The shepherd
guides them to the fountain of the water of life. Here in this
temple they are sheltered. God himself is their comforter.
With this revelation the vision of John is complete.

The coda expresses what it meant to the prophet to hope in
God and to hope in the power of the Lamb. Their sharing in
his Passion meant that this Shepherd would be present "day
and night" with these sheep. In their crying and in their

rejoicing, the heaven of the prophet's vision coincided with the earth of the martyrs' suffering.

There is still another significance to be observed in this picture of the Lamb shepherding his flock. As Jesus had sacrificed himself *for others,* the Christians to whom John disclosed this vision would vindicate their kinship with Jesus by comparable sacrifice *for others.* Only those saved by losing their lives could qualify for membership in the heavenly choir. In its earlier stage the vision had disclosed God's verdict on Christ's redefinition of poverty and wealth, of death and life. Now in its climax the vision disclosed Christ's verdict on those slaves who joined him in sacrifice for the sake of others. To feed the hungry, to provide homes for refugees, to comfort those who mourn—in such activities in an unredeemed world the prophet could hear the heavenly anthems. The vision becomes his confession of faith in the mission of a universal church that continues the redemptive suffering of the Lamb/Shepherd. To believe in the resurrection of Jesus is to believe in the ultimate validity of that mission.

● On completing this analysis of John's vision, the reader may wish to test it against the guidelines formulated in earlier chapters. Has the vision clarified the sense of divine vocation on the part of both the prophet and his audience? Has it enabled interpreters to make sense of that vocation by alerting them to the conflicts it provokes? Has it shown how those conflicts are episodes in the heavenly warfare between God and Satan, a warfare that points backward to primal beginnings and forward to final endings? (Cf. above, p. 31.) How does the vision embody John's prophetic vocation—to induce churches at worship to become more keenly aware of the gifts of the Spirit; to penetrate the protective shields of self-deception on the part of Christian congregations; to call disciples of Christ to renewed repentance for endemic blindness and deafness; to invite such reflection on the

Passion story of Jesus that they will be confronted with the nearness of his wrath and mercy? (Cf. above, p. 45.) Has the interpretation of John's message to his initial congregations made wise use of the symbolic values in Old Testament language, refusing to transpose ancient poetry into modern prose or to substitute modern measurements of time for biblical understandings of the relation of creation to Creator? Does listening to the prophet's vision enhance the perception of the deeper meanings that are intrinsic to the church's experience of such matters as sin and forgiveness, temptation and victory, blindness and its cure? (Cf. above, pp. 61-62.) We have not applied those guidelines in any perfunctory way, but we trust that, for some readers at least, the original vision may have come alive with new relevance and that the exposition will be convincing enough to demonstrate the falsity of many current and popular alternatives. The stock-in-trade of false prophets is to exploit for their own purposes the authentic visions of prophets like John.

5 THE DISCERNMENT OF THE SPIRIT IN BAPTISM
(1 Peter)

We have encountered in the Book of Revelation the visions and auditions of an apocalyptic prophet whose vocation impelled him to direct a message from the risen Christ to seven churches in Asia. The author of 1 Peter does not deal in such visions or auditions. Why, then, should we turn to his letter? It is true, of course, that he may on occasion have exercised the prophet's gift (1:1-12; 5:1-4). But here we are more concerned with audience than with author. How did the spiritual gifts received in their baptism enable believers to discern the revelations delivered to them by apostles and prophets? And does their discernment help us to interpret such revelations?

We have noted the common Christian assumption that whenever God spoke to his people, twin gifts came into play—a gift to the speaker and a gift to the listeners. We have also observed that this latter gift was supposed to be conveyed in baptism, an expectation persisting in modern liturgies, as illustrated by these petitions in the revised *Book of Common Prayer* of the Episcopal Church: "fill them with your holy and life-giving Spirit . . . "; "give them an inquiring and discerning heart . . . . " That prayer for a discerning heart may be taken as a matter of course or as a miraculous feature of new birth. In the New Testament the latter was the case. "The gift of discernment is basic to the genius of the biblical life-style . . . . (It) is the elementary, common and ecumenical gift, intrinsic to the authority which every Christian receives, essential to the use of all other charismatic gifts."[1]

First Peter is an excellent source for studying this spiritual gift, the twin to the gift of prophecy. It provides rather clear answers to the question: How does baptism convey the gift and how does its reception aid a congregation in discerning the revelations of its prophets?

> ● A warning must be issued: The term baptism will be misunderstood if we fill it with connotations drawn from modern theories and practices. Originally, Christian baptism marked a major revolution in the life of both individual and congregation. That revolution was accompanied by adoption into a new family and by vigorous hostility from neighbors (4:12-17). Those who were baptized entered a life whose horizons were defined by the resurrection from the dead (1:3) and by their vivid expectation of "the day of visitation" (2:12).

There are scholars who find within the Epistle a sermon (1:3; 4:11) originally addressed to a group of recent converts on the occasion, perhaps at Easter, of their baptism (F. L. Cross, F. W. Beare). Those converts have heard the good news proclaimed "through the Holy Spirit sent from heaven" (1:12). That news has become the "seed" of new birth, through which God has given them eternal life as his sons and daughters (1:23). Accordingly, when we read "baptism . . . *now* saves you" (3:21), we can almost hear a priest addressing a group of baptizands. That same accent on

[1]William Stringfellow, *An Ethic for Christians and Other Aliens in a Strange Land*, pp. 138, 141.

the *now* appears elsewhere (1:6, 8, 12; 2:10, 25), giving the impression that the listeners have only recently begun their exodus from earlier existence as pagans (1:1, 12, 14, 18; 2:9-12). The same kind of drastic transition is reflected by the dominant images: they are babes who have been born anew of incorruptible seed; like infants they must crave the "pure spiritual milk." Having recently shifted from darkness into the light of God's new creation, they have received the exalted vocation of a royal priesthood.

However, this view that the Epistle was based on a sermon delivered to baptizands is supported by only a minority of scholars. A slightly modified version does, in fact, win the support of a clear majority. Most commentators agree that a key objective of the letter was to clarify the significance of baptism as a new birth into a new family, and to stress the duties and potencies indigenous to this new mode of existence. This understanding of the Epistle encourages us to explore certain convictions with regard to baptism:

1. All who were baptized received charismatic gifts that marked a radical transition from old to new.
2. These gifts reflected apocalyptic perspectives, similar to those which we discover within the Book of Revelation.
3. The gifts enabled congregations to understand the purposes of God conveyed through the messages of prophets.

1. Where, then, may we locate clues to the charismatic gifts conveyed, according to this author, to all baptized Christians? In his opening greeting he specified that his readers, without exception, had become the objects and the recipients of divine action. God had chosen them, the Spirit had sanctified them, for obeying Jesus Christ. The commands of the risen Christ, relayed to them by his

messengers, had borne the stamp of the highest conceivable authority. That authority made clear the purpose of their calling: God had chosen them and the Spirit had sanctified them for "sprinkling with the blood of Jesus Christ." Their whole life now stood under the sign of the Cross. Their election pointed backward to the event of Jesus' death, and, in a mysterious way, it also pointed forward to a sprinkling with his blood. All charismatic gifts carried traces of this origin and goal.

For the period of his service, each Christian received a gift of God's grace and was appointed a steward of that grace (4:10, 11). Gifts were highly varied; the author distinguished, for example, the gift of uttering divine oracles from the gift of humble service. Three things could be said of all gifts: all were designed to glorify God; all were directed to benefitting other people; all could be exercized only through the strength supplied by God. Each flock had a shepherd, each shepherd a flock; each of these relied on the gift of humility toward the other (5:2-5). Whenever a prophet uttered the word of God's grace, listeners stood fast in that word (5:12).

The exercise of spiritual gifts continued throughout the time of their life, here called exile. The image—exile—indicated an apocalyptic conception of a double life: they existed in the dispersion as heirs of heaven. The spiritual gifts were links between that foreign domicile and the heavenly homeland.

• As modern interpreters we find it difficult to do full justice to this image of the church as composed of exiles, even though there are perhaps more exiles in the world today than ever before. However, the early Christians were all considered exiles *because* of their religious faith; it had alienated them all from the surrounding culture. Not many American Christians feel that same degree of alienation; they

therefore find little sense of kinship with the readers of 1
Peter. It is difficult to measure one's own sense of
at-homeness or away-from-homeness. Those who interpret 1
Peter belong perhaps to one of these three groups: those who
are at home in their own country, but not at home in any
other; those who are equally at home in their own and other
countries; those who are not at home in any country,
including their own. Only the last situation applied to the
author and readers of 1 Peter. Accordingly, perhaps the best
exegesis will come from those who feel themselves sharing
that situation.

During this double life, charismatic gifts were means by
which believers were being built into a "spiritual house"
where they offered "spiritual sacrifices" (2:5). In the phrase
"spiritual house," the adjective "designates not a method of
spiritualistic allegorization, but rather marks the house and
the sacrifices as objects of the creating and sustaining activity
of the Holy Spirit. He actualizes God's electing grace, builds
living stones into a Royal house, sanctifies the bodies of
priests, and makes their sacrifices acceptable."[2]
Within this house, the author distinguished the duties of
masters and slaves, husbands and wives. These distinctions
reflected current cultural attitudes, but it was also made clear
that the sufferings of Christ conveyed obligations that were
binding on all. The author recognized that husbands and
wives had different duties, but he insisted that they were
"joint-heirs of the grace of life" and that this common gift
enjoined them against taking any action that would hinder
their prayers (3:1-7). Together all Christians faced the risks
of persecution; their calling entailed a share in the sufferings
of Christ and in the sufferings of a worldwide brotherhood.
Such suffering became a test of the genuineness of their faith
and hope. "Persecution, with the temptation to apostasy, is

[2]John H. Elliott, *The Elect and the Holy* (Leiden: Brill, 1966), p. 196.

the atmosphere in which Christians permanently live."[3] To sum up, then, this Epistle provides us with numerous clues to the charismatic gifts which the author assumed to be active among baptized Christians in these five scattered provinces.

2. It should be clear that thinking about these gifts belonged within the context of apocalyptic perspectives characteristic of prophets like John. At the risk of undue repetition, let me itemize several features of those perspectives:

Item: All the gifts were viewed as coming from and pointing toward the activity of God, not a god in general but the very specific "father of our lord Jesus Christ." This remained the necessary frame of reference, without which all thoughts would have been truly senseless. "Blessed be the God . . . . To him be the dominion forever . . . . He who called you is holy . . . . [He] judges each impartially . . . . You are . . . God's own people . . . . [You] by God's power are guarded. . . . Your faith and hope are in God . . . . Live as servants of God." All such assertions reflect the same basic *theo*-logical perspective as the vision of John in Revelation 4.

Item: All gifts stem from what has been accomplished in the work of the Lamb that was slain. "Christ also suffered for you . . . . You were ransomed . . . with the precious blood of Christ, like that of a lamb" . . . He was destined before the foundation of the world but was made manifest at the end of the times for your sake . . . rejected by men but in God's sight chosen . . . [He] has gone into heaven and is at the right hand of God, with angels, authorities, and powers subject to him . . . . Set your hope fully upon the grace that is coming to you at the revelation of Jesus Christ." In Revelation 5 John saw the Lamb who had by his blood ransomed saints for

[3]John N. D. Kelly, *A Commentary on the Epistles of Peter and of Jude* (New York: Harper & Row, 1969), p. 9.

God and had made them a kingdom of priests. Peter did not describe such a vision, but he made clear to his readers that their baptism included them in the sufferings and glory on the part of the same Lamb, thus making them a royal priesthood.

Item: All gifts to the baptized carried the obligation to share in the sufferings of Christ. "Christ . . . suffered for you, leaving you an example . . . . Since Christ suffered in the flesh, arm yourselves with the same thought, for whoever has suffered in the flesh has ceased from sin . . . . Rejoice in so far as you share Christ's sufferings . . . . The genuineness of your faith . . . is tested by fire . . . . Conduct yourselves with fear throughout the time of your exile." Far from being alien to their vocation, suffering was something to be expected by all. As E. E. Best writes, "The background of the letter is thus persecution viewed from an eschatological perspective."[4] That perspective was not uncongenial to that of John, who saw under the heavenly altar the souls of those who had been killed and who saw on the throne a Shepherd feeding those who had washed their robes in the blood of the Lamb (Rev 6:9-11; 7:14-17).

Other links between John's visions and Peter's more sober advices can be mentioned without extended comment. Both authors recognize the devil as the chief adversary of Christ and his church. Both proclaim God's final judgment on abusers and persecutors. Both use the symbolic term *Babylon* without explanation. For both, the worship of the church provides the occasion for reflection on the elusive presence of God and the imperious commands of Christ. Both recognize the paradox of identifying the good shepherd with the slain Lamb, and the related paradox of identifying the "grace that is coming to you at the revelation of Jesus Christ" with their own acceptance of martyrdom. Both

[4] *1 Peter* (London: Oliphants, 1971), p. 14.

assume that the prophets of the old covenant had anticipated the suffering and glory of the Messiah; accordingly both feel free to link the present generation of believers to all former generations. We must repeat that 1 Peter is not an apocalypse but a letter of pastoral guidance. Even so, its conception of those charismatic gifts that attend baptism makes little sense in any context other than the apocalyptic.

3. Because this is true, those charismatic gifts helped readers of 1 Peter to comprehend messages of apocalyptic prophets like John. Baptism was clearly such an event as to separate Christians from non-Christians.

> ● Then as now this rule was applicable: "If you want to know the nature of the Church, you must not look at the point where it is most closely connected with its cultural environment!"[5] Baptism in the early church was an event that could be understood only by looking at points where the church was most decisively separated from its cultural environment.

As a consequence, the author of this epistle did not expect unconverted Gentiles to understand either the gifts or the messages (2:12). Most Gentiles would continue to stumble over the stone that the builders had rejected (2:7) and to abuse their Christian neighbors (4:3-5). By the same token the author expected those who had been baptized to understand both the gifts they had received and the events in heaven which those gifts reflected. Now we ask more specifically, how did those gifts help them understand the messages of the prophets, who had their own distinctive vocation?

It is a question difficult to answer, because the author himself did not give an explicit answer. We must read

[5]Gordon Rupp, *Last Things First* (Philadelphia: Fortress Press, 1964), p. 9.

between the lines to recover attitudes which he took for granted. We must be content with conjectures, among which three may be mentioned with a modest degree of probability.

Conjecture One emerges as we reflect upon those commands which this author relayed to his readers. The following commands are typical:

> Be subject to every human institution.
> Abstain from the passions of the flesh.
> Keep sane and sober for your prayers.
> Servants, be submissive to your masters.
> Honor the emperor.
> Seek peace and pursue it.
> Resist the devil.
> Do not return evil for evil.
> Rejoice insofar as you share Christ's sufferings.

Such commands may seem banal and bland until we recall that these Christians were undergoing the fiery ordeal of persecution. In that situation not one of these orders was easy to obey. We must also recall the vivid contrast between very visible enemies and altogether invisible forces. Each order was issued on the authority of a god wholly hidden from human eyes. Each carried the name of a savior who had been executed as enemy of the political and religious establishments. To obey any of the orders on the ground of this authority increased the dangers incurred by their faith, for obedience was a form of witnessing that the invisible God had in fact raised Jesus from the dead and had made all other powers and dominions subject to him (1:3; 3:21, 22). And this act of obedience was more than a mode of witnessing. It was inseparable from an act of comprehension. It was a believing response to the prophet's vision of the sovereignty of God, of the power awarded to the Lamb, of the souls of faithful saints under the altar, of victories won by servants of the Lamb. The act of obedience itself signaled the reality of the fellowship of saints and disclosed a divine grace operating at the center of earthly tragedy. *Conjecture One*, then, is this: the charismatic gifts embodied in baptism and made effectual by obedience to the authority of the heavenly Christ provided a hermeneutical key for unlocking apocalyptic prophecies, like those of John.

Conjecture Two emerges when we subject one of these commands to more detailed analysis. "Rejoice in so far as you share Christ's sufferings" (4:13). To avoid suffering is one line of action; voluntarily to accept suffering is action of a different order. To accept suffering, however slowly or quickly, is one thing; to accept suffering voluntarily as an innocent person suffering for the guilty is action of a yet different order. To do the latter is one thing (it may express a martyr-complex); to rejoice in that suffering is action of a yet different order. To do the latter is one thing (it may reveal a severe psychosis); to do it as a witness to the glory of God in Christ is action of a yet different order. These distinctions are important, and very difficult to make in practice.

In making this analysis we must remember that the suffering under discussion is real suffering. It is neither something imagined nor something limited to subjective feelings. And in Peter's judgment the rejoicing is just as real, nothing artificial or superficial, not a matter of forced good cheer. Joy is commanded under the assumption that those who have been baptized have the grace and the strength to obey. The more difficult the obedience, the more miraculous the joy. In this respect Peter's command to rejoice in suffering corresponds to John's vision of God wiping away "every tear from their eyes" (Rev 7:17). *Conjecture Two*: Those who in their baptism receive the grace to obey this command will discern many meanings in apocalyptic prophecy. For example, they will understand the Johannine

picture of divine judgment that begins with the household of
God and of crowns of glory awarded to the victors.

   Conjecture Three emerges as we consider still another
impossible command, "Do not return evil for evil."
Christians encountered enemies on all sides who were all too
ready to do them evil. Christian slaves faced retaliation by
brutal masters; believing wives faced the anger of unbelieving husbands; neighbors received all sorts of ridicule and
abuse from scornful neighbors; all risked condemnation in
the courts of the emperor. Yet the new master in heaven
required unqualified obedience to his command, which was
supported in various ways: by the example of Christ, by the
appeal to God's judgment, the only court where justice is
certain; by the desire to extend the chain of redemption, the
innocent suffering for the guilty. Inasmuch as the devil relied
upon the opposite rule—evil for evil—obedience to the
command signaled a dramatic shift in the balance of power
among the heavenly lords. The return of good for evil was
nothing less than a break in the vicious circle of demonic
retaliation, made possible by God's varied grace. Again we
may discern in this gift of grace a mode of understanding
apocalyptic prophecy, with its celebrations of Jesus' victory
over the dragon, its scenario of God's judgment of beasts and
false prophets (cf. our next chapter), its reliance on Jesus as
"the Shepherd and Guardian of your souls." There were
Christians, of course, who returned evil for evil; there would
otherwise have been no need for Peter's injunction. They
would presumably have misunderstood John's vision of
opening the seals (Revelation 6, 7). But those who obeyed
the order to return good for evil would be able to grasp the
reasons why the Lamb had received authority to open the
scroll. *Conjecture Three*: The action of returning good for
evil represented a profound understanding of the prophet's
vision of the victory of Christ. Here again the inner theater
would correspond to the outer theater; Christian obedience

would become the act by which a reader would hear the same commands as the prophet (e.g., John) had heard issuing from the throne of God and the Lamb. Such obedience represented a victory over the devil made possible by Jesus' victory in such a way that all such victories could be visualized by the prophet as one victory.

> ● We should not forget that whether this Epistle began its life as a sermon addressed to recent converts undergoing baptism or as a letter to churches scattered through five provinces, it would certainly have been read aloud in gatherings for worship. In that reading the letter would have intensified the God-church dialogue, from the opening "Blessed be the God . . . " to the closing "Peace to all of you who are in Christ." The dynamics of thought would have become welded into the dynamics of praise and thanksgiving. The moral difficulties, the historical dilemmas, the ecclesiastical tensions—these would have found silent expression in prayers and sacraments under the guidance of the Holy Spirit. In this respect the Epistle reminds us of the relevance of Guidelines 6 and 15 as defined in chaps. 2 and 3.

In conclusion, we note that although at many points all baptized Christians were treated as recipients of the same basic vocation as the prophet, 1 Peter preserves a significant distinction between those believers and their prophetic leaders. By implication this distinction comes to the surface in 1:8: "Without having seen him you love him; though you do not now see him you believe in him and rejoice with unutterable and exalted joy." In these words the author implies that members of the churches have not seen the risen Lord in the same way as those who had been commissioned by him as apostles (cf. John 20:29). He may also imply that those members do not now see the risen Lord in the same way as prophets who, like John in Revelation chaps. 1 and 5, continue to have visions of the Lamb whose sufferings serve as the paradigm for their own exile. For them the visions of the prophet are not an essential gift; this fact, however, makes all the more essential such gifts as joy, hope, love, and endurance. Because prophets are eyewitnesses of the sufferings and glory of Christ, they have authority to testify to the crown of glory which faithful shepherds will receive when the chief shepherd is manifested (5:1, 5).

6   A VISION OF HEAVENLY WARFARE
(Revelation 11:19–14:5)

In returning to the apocalyptic prophecies of John we will examine a vision that has caused interpreters great difficulties. Not least is the difficulty of anchoring this vision in the situation in the churches of Asia. In all probability the Book of Revelation began its life as a series of prophecies originally delivered in person to those congregations during their services of worship. John's work as a prophet was one reason for his arrest and imprisonment (Rev 1:9). That imprisonment, in which John himself had to fight his own battle with Satan, gave him an opportunity to write down those earlier prophecies, to edit them into a single narrative, and to send that collection of visions to the seven churches. (Because seven was a symbolic number indicating completeness, it is probable that John intended an even larger audience, perhaps as large as that of 1 Peter.)

This vision began at 11:19 with the opening of God's temple in heaven where the ark of the covenant became visible. This location is important, for it reveals the prophet's concern to disclose those realities that were implicit in the agelong worship of Israel.

• The three images—temple, ark, covenant—serve to alert readers to the fact that the prophet is drawing upon his

91

dictionary of Old Testament symbols (cf. Guideline 11). Accordingly, students should at this point consult a concordance or Bible dictionary to learn the traditional force of these images. Since these images are seen in heaven, it is clear that the prophet is giving a poetic and parabolic force to them (Guideline 12). He is dealing with realities that "require a mythology for their adequate expression and cannot influence the conduct of men until they have bodied forth in powerful imaginative symbols."[1] Such metaphors derive their complex meanings from traditional use in worship (Guidelines 2, 6).

The same concern is apparent in the climax of the vision in 14:1-5. Here the Lamb is pictured with his faithful followers, joining with their harps and hymns in the worship already described in chap. 7 (above, pp. 69 ff.). These followers have been redeemed; the mark of that redemption is victory over the kind of self-deception that would have induced them to betray their allegiance to the Lamb. In other words, the vision ends with the fulfillment of their calling, when they have truly entered God's temple and have proved themselves worthy of the same covenant that had supported Israel throughout its wilderness wanderings.

When we give full weight to this setting in worship, with a Spirit-inspired speaker addressing a Spirit-inspired congregation, we realize that we are dealing with a vision and not with some other form of communication. The prophet's vision is designed to help that congregation see features in their situation which otherwise would remain hidden. If this were not so, there would be no sense whatever in his calling.

● In Revelation, the previous segment deals more explicitly with John's own calling (10:8–11:8). There he was com-

[1]G. B. Caird, *A Commentary on the Revelation of St. John the Divine* (New York: Harper & Row, 1966), pp. 148.

manded to prophesy to a very large audience with
instructions to measure the temple and its altar, an altar
defined by those who worship there. John's vision of warfare
in heaven comes as his effort to accomplish that assignment.

Because this prophecy takes the form of a vision we should
not turn it into an allegory, an algebraic formula in which we
may detect a one-to-one correspondence between each
detail in the vision and a corresponding historical entity. This
heaven is not equivalent to the sky across which clouds scud,
nor is this earth the location of Route #1 between New York
and Philadelphia. The vision has its own integrity as a vision;
it is not a secret code with an open invitation to ingenious
interpreters to crack it. We do not make contact with the
prophet's mind by reducing each figure in his narrative to
some empirical equivalent, e.g., the beast is the Roman
empire. The dangers of such decoding are illustrated in a
fantastic anecdote. A museum in Egypt once displayed a
clump of dusty bones with the legend: "These are the bones
of the seven lean cattle that devoured the seven fat cattle
(Gen 41:1-8)." For weeks gullible tourists viewed the exhibit
with expressions of appropriate awe until one of them, better
acquainted with Genesis than the others, hooted with
unbelief: "But those cattle were only figures in Pharaoh's
dream." Although a prophet's vision is not the same as a
dream, it is like a dream in that the substitution of a visible
equivalent for each invisible item is a mistake.

The vision at hand depicts a war that arose in heaven. In
this war, action shifts from one front to another. The first
battle is fought between a woman garbed in the sun and a
great red dragon. The woman's goal is to give birth to a child,
the dragon's is to devour that child (12:1-6). The woman
wins. The child is caught up to God, to his throne, where he
rules all the nations with a rod of iron. "The woman is the
mother of the Messiah, not Mary, but the messianic

community. . . . The agony of her labor is the suffering
endured by the loyal people of God as they waited for their
anointed king. . . . By the birth of the Messiah, John means
not the Nativity but the Cross. . . . He is continuing his
exposition of the second psalm. . . . Satan thought that death
was the means by which Jesus would come permanently
within his power, when in fact it was the means by which he
was carried forever beyond his power."[2]

The second battle involves a wider set of adversaries
(12:7-12). The archangel Michael with armies of angels is set
against the same dragon (now identified as the Serpent, the
devil, and Satan) with his angelic cohort. In this case
Michael's army wins the day. John gives two important clues
to the opposing strategies. The dragon relies on deception,
and his strategy is widely successful. He seeks to deceive
"our brethren" by accusing them before "our God." On his
part, Michael appeals to the salvation and the royal power of
"our God" and to "the authority of his Christ." Michael's
strategy wins, but only when servants of the Lamb are ready,
in their allegiance to him, to forfeit their own lives.

The adversaries are different, but the opposing strategies
are the same. This means that the warfare between the
woman and Michael, on one hand, and the devil with his
troops, on the other, becomes a way of articulating the inner
struggles of those Christians who stand on the battle lines. It
is as if they asked: "How can we penetrate the deceptive
strategies of the ancient serpent and defeat him?" An answer
is given in the third act of the drama, where the scene shifts to
the wilderness, ancient symbol of the place of maximum
temptation and the place where the God of Israel provides
food and guidance. The devil remains enemy number one;
he can draw on awesome resources in a flood. Yet the woman
remains steadfast, aided by an eagle. The devil shifts his

[2]Ibid., pp. 149-51.

onslaught against "the rest of her offspring," but his devices are futile against "those who keep the commandments of God and bear testimony to Jesus." In this wilderness, the victory of the woman becomes inseparable from their victory.

That victory, however, prompts the Serpent to call to his aid two puppet-beasts. The first, a sea-beast, turns his wiles against the same foes, the saints (13:1-10). He calls into play all the symbols of royal authority that had been claimed by the Serpent. His objective is to persuade saints to worship both him and the dragon; he could reach this goal only by deceiving those saints with regard to the power of this counterfeit god. He did in fact succeed in conquering saints and securing world-wide worship of this blasphemous substitute for the true God. Yet there were saints who displayed enough courage and endurance to repel this subtle temptation.

A more deceptive puppet was therefore needed. The second puppet, an earth-beast, was authorized by the first beast to persuade the saints to worship him. A master of deceit, this second beast spoke with the authority of the dragon, even though it had the horns of a lamb (13:11-18). Masked in innocence, it yet was the spokesman of evil. It produced impressive credentials, working signs that seemed to reflect divine approval. It even exerted power to raise the first beast from death and to destroy those who would not recognize that power by worshiping the beast and, through him, the dragon. In fact, it claimed the power to murder those who refused such worship (the same power described in 12:4). (In later visions, John spoke of this earth-beast as a false prophet—19:20; 20:10.).

Yet all these strategies failed. On Mt. Zion, John saw the true Lamb and all those whom the Lamb had ransomed, those who had not been trapped into worshiping these false but powerful gods (14:1-5). So the climax of the war is reached not in a negotiated treaty or in a stalemate, but in the singing of hymns before the throne. The choristers are those "who follow the Lamb wherever he goes." They have penetrated the deceptions of the Dragon and his puppets, have refused to revere their power. There has been in their confessions of faith no hypocrisy or duplicity; "In their mouth no lie was found."

Although the main thrust of the message of John to his churches is clear, there remain many difficulties in interpreting the details. Those difficulties are almost always accentuated by a persistent temptation of interpreters to identify themselves and their own favored human community with the woman and her children, and to think of their specific human enemies as tools of the serpent and his puppets. When they use such reasoning, interpreters learn nothing from John's vision except the ratification of their own prejudices as defined by their own group-interest. If the first readers of John had done this, they would have learned nothing from him.

For avoiding this exercise in ventriloquism, three guidelines may be helpful. The first is #6: the interpreter of charismatic gifts must participate in the dynamics of Christian worship as it opens the gates of heaven and affords prophets an opportunity to relay messages from God. We should be content with no interpretation that is inherently uncongenial to this setting. Unfortunately, the interpretations most popular in the modern scene are prime examples of uncongeniality. Contrariwise, we should stress those aspects of John's message that are congenial to a worship setting. This standard of judgment might well lead us to ask such questions as the following:

Which of the many gods is worthy to be worshiped?

Which are the gods competing for that worship?

How does worship reflect estimates of power?

How can worshipers avoid deceiving themselves in worship?

How does a community become qualified to worship the true God?

What forms of worship are compatible with the ways in which the Lamb won his victory?

How may false prophecy be distinguished from true?

When we ask such questions in all seriousness, John's vision of warfare in heaven can become highly relevant.

A second guideline comes into play when we notice a second recurrent motif in the vision. Satan is recognized as "the deceiver of the whole world," the ultimate source of the "lie" (12:9; 14:5). To overcome his seductions, Christians must become adept at self-examination. This is the point at which the role of prophets becomes essential, the point where Guideline 7 becomes pertinent. Prophets must penetrate the masks of hypocrisy within their communities and their interpreters must aid them. In terms of apocalyptic idiom they must, in warning against fornication, secure the chastity of those who have pledged to follow the Lamb wherever he goes, even to a cross. Like their master, they must insist on the truth that no one can serve two masters, and they must do this in a community where everyone is in fact serving many masters. This battle between truth and the lie continues day after day, the agelong battle between God and Satan. A secular recognition of the urgency of this battle comes from Sartre in his statement that self-deception "is an immediate permanent threat to every project of the human being."[3]

We have noticed how John's vision instructs his readers concerning the increasing subtlety of the enemy. The devil has discovered that a frontal attack on the saints leads to their victory (12:8-11), so he resorts to the use of puppets who are more expert in deception, the sea-beast and the

[3]Cited by Stephen Crites, *Soundings* 61 (1979): 107-10.

earth-beast. Their ability to recover from a mortal wound, combined with their power to inflict death, enables them to deceive "those who dwell on earth." The result is idolatry and blasphemy among those pledged to serve God rather than Caesar, Mammon, or self. Consequently we are bound to distort John's thought unless we recall that he was speaking to secret places of the heart where a community's ultimate loyalties are decided, and unless we ourselves grapple with the protean forms of hypocrisy.

John's vision clarifies the area where such deceitfulness achieves its maximum effectiveness—the point where power is manifested. This fact accounts for the elaborate descriptions of the dragon: he has seven heads, ten horns, and seven diadems upon his heads. He exerts enough power to sweep the very stars from heaven. His authority appears to extend over every tribe, nation, linguistic and cultural community. The shorter the time, the greater his wrath. The more resistance to his claims, the more he turns his weapons against dissenters. He secures his objective when people cry: "Who is like the beast, and who can fight against it?" The key question has to do with the balance of power. Here, as elsewhere, the interpreter of apocalyptic prophecy must be sensitive to the ways in which the historical conflicts which result from a community's vocation are repercussions of a more ultimate conflict between one God and other gods (Guideline 4).

In the heart of that community an answer has to be given to the questions: Who exerts greater power over the future, the pregnant woman or the devouring dragon? Which has the more effective army, Michael or the devil? Who will inherit the temple in heaven, children of the woman or worshipers of the beast? Those are not idle questions, precisely because the present seems to be wholly under the control of Satan, because he appears to have the control over life and death, and because his prophets, in working his signs, can identify the self-interest of the churches with obeisance before these lords.

In every generation, including the first, interpreters are tempted to locate the ultimate enemies of the churches in some visible entity, a particular nation or race or economic or religious system, ignoring the fact that, while those who wield power over others are always visible, the source of their power is always invisible. To treat human enemies as ultimate enemies constitutes deception of the first order. To defeat such human enemies or to be defeated by them is *not* the definition of victory or defeat that John had in mind. Communities adopt such goals without help from prophets. Only when the enemies are invisible, and when a community is deceived by them, is the work of a prophet essential. He must bring a word from the only god who can rightly claim to be almighty.

Let us then sum up our answer to the question of how noncharismatic interpreters can grasp the force of this charismatic vision of the war in heaven: by due regard for the dynamics of Christian worship and, in this case, the worship of a community undergoing extreme hostility. By sensitivity to the inner struggles between integrity and hypocrisy, struggles that could only be fought within the secret ventricles of the heart. By awareness of the degree to which psychic and moral struggles are inseparable from historical and cosmic manifestations of power. All these struggles seem to come to a focus in the question of which gods are to be worshiped, in a situation in which one kind of power is expressed in murder and its opposing power in willingness to be murdered. In their effort to interpret a vision of this sort, students are themselves involved in that complex cluster of struggles.

But we must return to the churches of Asia and ask how the Spirit through the prophet would help them identify their most dangerous adversaries. There is some evidence that

John's description of the sea-beast would have conjured up in their minds the tremendous power of the Roman empire. The earth-beast may have prompted them to think of hostile members of the synagogue who often informed against Christians in connection with official trials. The earth-beast has also been linked to the priests of the imperial cult, persuading residents of the empire to worship the deified emperor. To some interpreters that beast may have been operating through "false" Christian prophets who counseled the churches to accede to the idolatrous commands of synagogue or empire. The letters to the seven churches provide basis for all these identifications, for in them the prophet speaks of officially sanctioned executions, of the hostility of synagogues, and of prophetic descendants of Balak, Balaam, and Jezebel.

But such direct identifications of the animals in this heavenly zoo seems to be secondary to John's major intentions. To him all the current battles are seen as contemporary revivals of a war that had been fought earlier at the time of the Exodus, or when Israel was living in the wilderness, or when the Messiah carried out his mission, and wherever servants of that Messiah confronted the devil's anger. Just as the devil is the deceiver not of one nation alone, but of the whole world, so, too, any membership in the family of the messianic mother makes participation in this warfare inescapable.

Of all the criteria that would enable readers to identify both sides in this warfare, the most decisive to John was the story of Jesus, and especially the centrality in that story of the "blood of the Lamb." It was the identity of this child that determined the identity of the mother, as well as of the rest of her offspring. It was the identity of this Lamb-Lion that determined the identity of all the opposing forces, the demonic trinity of dragon, sea-beast, and earth-beast. John's analysis of cosmic power was anchored in his appraisal of the forces that secured the death of Jesus, as well as of the forces at work in his victory. For him, these identifications and appraisals took the form not of conjecture and speculation, but of obedience and action. It was by their action that the churches in Asia witnessed to the power of Lamb or dragon. So it was the story of Jesus that ultimately made it impossible for the churches to identify good or evil wholly with human enemies or friends; and that same story disclosed the self-deception at work in all measurements of power that did not recognize "the rod of iron" with which this Messiah was authorized to rule the nations. In short, the difficulties in understanding this vision are best approached by recognizing the relevance of Guideline 10: An interpreter of Christian prophecy must become alert to the multiple ways in which the charismatic utterance of the prophet and the charismatic response of the worshiping congregation were aspects of their joint response to the story of Jesus, as focused in his death and resurrection, and as those events became contemporaneous through the prophet's work.

In this vision, then, John, as an apocalyptic prophet, was disclosing to the churches in Asia the range of cosmic powers which had been active in the story of Jesus, which had become present in a hidden form in the solidarity that bound these Christians to the sufferings of their Lord, and which were daily seeking to deceive them through apparent control over both the present and the future.

7 THE DISCERNMENT OF THE SPIRIT IN SHARED FUTILITY
(Romans 8)

John's vision of a war in heaven, which we have been examining, seems unlike anything else in the New Testament because of its surrealist nightmares of fighting dragons and beasts. That zoo seems remote even from John's earlier letters to the seven churches, though the prophet's objectives in both visions were much the same. When we turn to Romans 8 we encounter material that seems so remote that few readers see any connection. In form, of course, Romans is not an apocalypse. Nevertheless, the shape and force of Paul's argument spring from an apocalyptic conception of the conflicts inherent in the vocation of the apostle and of his readers. And Paul was acutely aware that spiritual discernment was needed if readers were to understand those conflicts. One circumstance made Paul's task more difficult than John's: in the letter to the Romans, Paul was writing to congregations which he had not yet visited. Moreover his letter reveals the fact that both he and his readers had received highly negative reports about each other.

It is well at the outset to observe that although Paul spoke of himself as an apostle, this vocation was itself grounded in the gift of prophecy. In the opening verses of the Epistle,

Paul traces his own commission to the chain of God's promises through prophets. He described his call in a way comparable to Isaiah and Jeremiah: "When he who had set me apart before I was born, and had called me through his grace, was pleased to reveal his Son to me, in order that I might preach him among the Gentiles . . ." (Gal 1:15; cf. Isa 49:1-6; Jer 1:4-5). In his disclosures of God's will Paul often used the language of visionary experience (1 Cor 7:10; 9:1; 11:23; 14:37-38; 15:8; 2 Cor 12:2-4, 7; Gal 2:1-2; 1 Thes 4:13-17).

There is no mistaking the sense of authority that underlies the Epistle to the Romans. Paul made his appeal according to "the grace given me by God" (15:15). He appealed to the Holy Spirit as the seal of his honesty. When he came to deal with the future destiny of unbelieving Israel, he disclosed "a mystery," making direct use of a prophetic way of speaking (11:25). The same idiom permeated the revelation of both God's wrath and his grace (1:16-18). The very writing of the letter was an effort to accomplish a mission which he had received from the risen Lord (1:4-6).

● Readers may well question the identification of Paul as an apocalyptic prophet, so deeply engrained is the habit of thinking of him only as an apostle. Moreover, they may remember that on occasion Paul distinguished the gift of apostleship from the gift of prophecy (1 Cor 12:28; Eph 4:11). And it must be conceded that Paul nowhere explicitly spoke of himself as a prophet. Yet he came very close to that in his discussion of the prophetic gift in 1 Corinthians (13:2; 14:6-19) and there are sections in his letters that are universally recognized as apocalyptic in form and style (e.g., 1 Thessalonians 4, 5). The distinction which Paul drew was a necessary one inasmuch as not all prophets in his day were apostles, sent by the risen Lord to spread the gospel to the unconverted and to supervise fledgling congregations. But the treatment of Paul as a prophet is also necessary inasmuch

as all apostles were prophets. The definition of this spiritual
gift with which we have been working (cf. above, pp. 29-30)
applies clearly to the author of Romans.

And what about his readers? Throughout the letter Paul
took it for granted that they had received a wide range of
spiritual gifts (12:1-8). They had died with Christ that they
might share his resurrection. As in 1 Peter, baptism was
viewed as marking new birth, the transition from death to life
(6:1-14). The argument of chap. 8 presupposed that readers
had covenanted to live according to the Spirit and had
adopted a new set of the mind and a new way of walking
(8:1-6). The Spirit of life in Christ Jesus had, in fact, become
their Law. Author and readers had never met; yet Paul
stressed their kinship as "fellow heirs with Christ" (8:17).

Because of this kinship, the prophet-apostle was concerned to disclose the ultimate dimensions of their common
hope (8:24), making clear its invisible origins as well as the
future to which it pointed. Nor was this hope a private "in
house" peculiarity. It involved God's design for creation as a
whole, a design that comprehended creation's present
futility and bondage to decay as well as its coming
redemption. That inclusive redemption was in fact assured
by "the glory that is to be revealed to us" (8:18). In all these
matters Paul was speaking as one who had been qualified by
the Spirit to receive and to disclose divine secrets.

In all this activity, to be sure, the apostle was not
interested in cosmic speculation or in impressive rhetoric.
He was concerned with meeting more immediate urgencies.
The focus of that concern comes to the surface most clearly in
his citation of Ps 44:22: "For thy sake we are being killed all
the day long; we are regarded as sheep to be slaughtered."
That citation is of first importance. We recall that one task of
a prophet was the reinterpretation of Scripture to show its
relevance to current happenings. In this case, the prophet

discerned a hidden connection between "the sufferings of this present time" and earlier afflictions that had induced Israel to suppose that God had gone to sleep. In this quotation, Paul intended the *we* to refer to servants of God in many generations, including the apostle himself and members of the churches in Rome. The phrase *all the day long* pointed to the cumulative experience of centuries, just as the phrase *for your sake* focused attention not on all human injustices but on martyrdoms incurred in line of loyalty to the "God of our fathers." So, too, the reference *sheep* called to the minds of Roman readers both "the Lamb that was slain" at a particular Passover and the flock of that particular shepherd (cf. 1 Pet 2:21-25; Rev 13:8). Skeptical readers may find in this interpretation of the Psalm a tendency to exaggerate the sufferings of Roman Christians; but such readers should recall that the Neronic pogrom against those same Christians occurred only a few years after this Epistle was written.

Paul was no hypochondriac, but a hard-nosed realist who was forced to deal with actual conditions, both in Corinth, where he was writing, and in Rome, to which he was writing. In both cities Christians were being forced to reckon with "distress, or persecution, or famine, or nakedness, or peril or sword" (8:35). Moreover, Paul had become qualified to deal with such things, qualified by "countless beatings, often near death . . . five times the thirty-nine lashes, three times beaten with rods, once stoned, three times shipwrecked . . . dangers from robbers, from my own people, from Gentiles, from false brethren . . . through many sleepless nights . . . in hunger and thirst . . . in cold and exposure" (2 Cor 11:23-29). How quickly that list can be read, and how quickly forgotten! But what endurance such experiences must have demanded! It was such a chain of crises that may have come to Paul's mind when he wrote about "being killed all the day long." Personal struggles of this intensity had inducted him

into knowledge of a creation subjected to futility and to
bondage to decay.

It is also clear that, in writing Romans 8, Paul included his
readers among those who shared in that futility, that
bondage. So we may well ask how they had participated in
his adversities. Had they encountered dangers like his from
Israelites, from Gentiles, from false brethren? We cannot
speak here with confidence because direct evidence is
lacking. We have no epistle from the Romans with accounts
of lashings and stonings. To be sure, Paul orders them to
"bless those who persecute you," and he prohibits any taking
of vengeance (12:14, 19). Such teachings may have been
perfunctory and customary, but they would have been
pointless if these readers had been entirely free from
persecution. In chap. 8, however, Paul seems to have had in
mind much less dramatic if no less dangerous enemies. Some
Roman Christians were encountering hostility from the
synagogues not unlike that experienced by Jesus and his
witnesses elsewhere. Only thus would Paul have casually
identified these Jews as "enemies of God, for your sake"
(11:28).

We must also ask what lies behind Paul's assertion that
"there is therefore now no condemnation for those who are
in Christ Jesus" (8:1). Probably he had in mind Jewish
Christians who were saying to Gentile Christians in effect,
"There is now nothing but condemnation for you if you fail
to live by the Torah." There is little doubt that this was
precisely the attitude of many Jewish Christians toward
Gentile believers (14:3, 10, 13). They were certain that
God's verdict would go against all who did not obey laws
regulating Sabbath observance and dietary purity. They
were saying "the Law's requirements are just," and there
can be no salvation for those who ignore them. Against them
Paul countered: "Of course those commands are just, but as
long as we were in the flesh we could not obey them. God has

now done what the Law could not do. The Spirit has enabled us to meet his requirements. But you set yourselves against God when you cancel out what he has done in Christ and when you reject the power of the Spirit. You have made yourselves slaves to the flesh, to the law of sin and death, because you are yourselves unable to fulfill the demands of the Law. Over against your reliance on the Law we must stand by what God has done." "If the Spirit of him who raised Jesus from the dead dwells in you, he who raised Christ Jesus from the dead will give life to your mortal bodies also through the Spirit which dwells in you" (8:11).

To sum up our argument thus far, three points are basic: Paul and the believers in Rome had received a common vocation from God through the death and resurrection of Christ, conveyed through the gift of the Spirit. This vocation had precipitated a wide range of conflicts within and outside the community of believers. Those conflicts, in turn, had established an axis that linked the sufferings of the community to the futility of creation as a whole. These points forced Paul to reflect upon the problem of the ultimate origins of that futility. How are we to identify the ultimate 110enemies of God, of Christ, of the Spirit, and therefore of the community that has received its vocation from the Spirit?

It is as an answer to this question that Paul's statement in 8:38 becomes very important, with its nine specific options:

death	life	
angels	principalities	
things present	things to come	
powers	heights	depths

This list would seem to include all potential enemies; but to make it complete the apostle added "anything else in all creation." By demonstrating the futility of human desires and goals, anything in creation can become an enemy. In one way or another all of these entities can resist and defeat human programs of action. We must note that no human individual or group is included in that list. This omission is specially noteworthy from the pen of an author who had suffered so much from so many different groups.

Paul's Roman readers were more prone to trace their frustrations to human adversaries. To some of them, Jews in the synagogues represented the chief enemies; to some of them, it was the group of Gentile Christians who flouted the authority of the Law; to some, it was the group of Jewish Christians who refused to associate with them. Not only were these human groups "our enemies"; they must also be considered "God's enemies," separated from God's love and from his plan of salvation. Given these frozen identifications, the momentum of hostility could only go on mounting steadily. Those who were content with such identifications would be unaware of any need for prophecy. But if the ultimate enemies belonged to a different order, to nonhuman and superhuman forces, then the twin gift of prophecy and of the discernment of prophecies became absolutely necessary. One of the major functions of Romans 8 was to disclose to Roman Christians the precise location and character of their real enemies.

> ● One should ask why it was that Paul viewed all creation as subject to futility. An answer would surely include reference to the sin and death that Paul traced back to the primeval fall. Humanity since that fall has been prone to dream of earthly futures in terms of present hopes and fears. A modern term covering this dream in its totality is futurology. Not only is futurology shaped by human desires for individual and group fulfillment; it is also an expression of human will-to-power, the effort to gain control over the future and to shape it in ways conducive to survival and to superiority over human competitors. Because of its origin in rebellion of creation against the creator, such futurology engenders illusion and despair. It reveals a slavery to "things present [and] things to

come." As a prophet Paul discerned in the action of Christ the gift of freedom from that futility.

In this respect Paul's prophecy, like John's, was grounded in an understanding of the invisible heavenly forces that had seemed to defeat the mission of Jesus, and of the resources that had enabled Jesus to win a decisive victory over those forces (cf. above, pp. 100-101). Ultimate futility and ultimate triumph had been disclosed when God "did not spare his own Son but gave him up for us all" (8:32). Apparent weakness in the face of Jesus' human enemies had concealed a strength in the face of his invisible foes. And it was that strength that had been revealed in the resurrection, and been made available to believers through the Spirit. Like John, Paul attached one condition: "provided we suffer with him [Christ]" (8:17).

It was because of Jesus' victory over these principalities and powers (cf. the demonic trinity in Rev 13:13) that there could be no condemnation for those who are in Christ Jesus. Charges could be brought against them by their human enemies, but none of those charges would be sustained in the court of last appeal. In their resistance to God's design, these enemies might even be called enemies of God, but in that case Christians must recognize that they have become enemies of God "for your sake" (11:28), and that therefore Christians must bless them. Such a response to human enemies would itself become a witness to Christ's victory over all superhuman enemies. That victory had been revealed in the exaltation of Christ to the right hand of God, where he "intercedes for us," that is, where he shares his power over these enemies with all who in sharing Christ's weakness also reflect the futility of all creatures. In short, the correct identification of enemies becomes absolutely essential, and in that identification the twin gifts of the Spirit come into play. From this approach, many of the assertions in Romans 8 become more intelligible:

—Weakness in dealing with human enemies is precisely the situation when the Spirit, which is both within us and at the throne of God, intercedes for us (vv 26-27).

—Because we have been predestined to bear the image of God's Son, every current peril can prove God's power to bring good out of evil, and thus to show both his primal grace and his final glory (vv 28-29).

—No distress attending his call can separate us from Christ's love because it was in fact his death that proved God's love for us (vv 31-32).

—It is the Holy Spirit within us that produces courage and confidence that "things to come" cannot separate us from the love of Christ (vv 9-10).

—Children of God who look forward toward the redemption of their bodies are evidence that the whole creation, subjected to futility, can look forward to a glorious liberty (vv 18-19).

—The Spirit of life in Christ Jesus has set Israel free from bondage to the Law which, intended as witness to God's grace, had become another sign of creation's futility (vv1-2).

—This freedom from the Law is the very fulfillment of the Law; those who believe that the Law can separate believers from the love of God are themselves slaves to the law of sin and death (vv 3-4).

—In response to adversaries in Israel, Christians must respond not with hatred, but with great sorrow and a sincere desire to be accursed for their sake (9:1-2).

When one examines the whole clump of corollaries of Paul's argument in this chapter, looking for the essential nucleus that holds them together, the following conclusions become inescapable: If in his Passion, Christ had not overcome all the potential sources of creation's futility, as listed in 8:38, 39, none of these corollaries would have been left intact. Moreover, if the Spirit of the God who had raised Jesus from the dead had not been given to Paul and to his Christian readers, it would be folly to trust any of these assertions. Contrariwise, if those two conditions are granted, the corollaries must stand. And for the author of this Epistle, the response of the readers was extremely important. His whole case rested on a confirmation by the Spirit that had been given to them. Only if that gift confirmed his announcement of Christ's victory over all the forces that held creation in bondage would they be able to discern the truth.

Having reviewed the structure of Paul's argument, we should now compare it with that of John in his vision of warfare in heaven. In many respects a reader may see virtually no connection; the surface contrasts are simply too great. Yet when we turn attention to the ways in which each prophet fulfilled his vocation, we may discover deep-lying congenialities. Both were primarily involved in meeting emergencies within the congregations for which they felt responsible. Both became aware of a significant axis between those emergencies and the sufferings of Jesus. Both traced the origin of the conflicts between saints and their human adversaries to vast invisible forces, so that human hostilities were to be understood as repercussions of an ultimate conflict between God and his heavenly adversaries. In both cases, the community of Christians had been divided, and these divisions had been aggravated by competing leaders who defended their partisan positions by appeal to Scriptures and to the gospel. Both prophets discerned unexpected ties between this internal Christian situation and the struggles endemic to the whole of creation. Neither prophet permitted fellow-believers in those internal or external altercations to return evil for evil or to give way to despair. Neither could be accused of romantic reduction of the odds facing the churches; neither could accept any ultimate limitation to the power of Christ. For both, kinship to Christ included kingship with him.

> • This comparison of the two documents illustrates a long-standing principle of interpretation: insofar as possible, Scripture should be interpreted by Scripture. By giving an independent picture of Christ's struggle with the "powers," Paul suggests the psychological and historical relevance of John's more colorful pictures of the war in heaven. Or in reverse, John's pictures provide a visual version of how God's decision not "to spare his Son" had created a new alignment in human affairs. The two different ways of dealing with creation's bondage to decay accentuate their united witness to the victory of the Lamb.

This interpretation of the thought of John and Paul may cast light on subsequent historical as well as theological developments of the period. Early Christianity was an apocalyptic movement that demonstrated an explosive force equaled by few other movements in human history. Within two or three decades it attracted massive hostilities, of which Paul's statement "we are regarded as sheep to be slaughtered" was a mild description. Simultaneously it attracted the most fervent loyalties, of which the assertion "we are more than conquerors" is a mild echo. This phenomenal force calls for some explanation.

Undoubtedly such an explanation must weave together many interacting influences—psychic, moral, political, economic, cultural, as well as intellectual and spiritual. Mysteries are involved here that defy the best analysis of historical process. Yet among these influences, it would be shortsighted to ignore the impact of apocalyptic thought itself. How much weight should be given to the realistic appraisal, shared by John and Paul, of the futility and bondage experienced by creation as a whole? How much weight should be given to their tracing of this bondage to heights and depths that far transcend human control and that are indifferent to human manipulation? Were these men right in detecting in the story of Jesus' crucifixion a collision between irresistible forces and an immovable object? Were they right in relating that collision to the abysmal range of human agonies and anxieties and to the stubborn resistance of every establishment—whether religious, economic, or political—to any creative intervention on the part of the Creator? Did their witness to the victory of Christ over "anything in all creation" that might separate people from the love of God produce such corroboration from human hearts as to release unparalleled excitements and dreads? There is a point where the historical riddle of which we have spoken meets the theological riddle, a point where the impact of prophetic revelation (apocalypse) must be credited with producing a revolution in human history. That is the point where a noncharismatic interpreter must deal with the charismatic visions of John and Paul, and with Paul's insistence that all who are led by the Spirit of God are sons of God (8:14) freed from the law of sin and death. The experience of such freedom is surely one ingredient in the explosive force exhibited by the early Christian movement.

How are we to explain the fervent loyalties and the fanatic hostilities released by the early Christian movement? I am convinced that no explanation is adequate that does not do justice to the character of Christianity as an apocalyptic movement, grounded in apocalyptic thought. This thought, in turn, was an articulation of apocalyptic visions through which both prophet and people received an utterly decisive sense of vocation. Neither loyalties nor hostilities can be explained apart from recognizing the power inherent in this new awareness.

Do contemporary historians give an adequate explanation of those hostilities and loyalties? The answer must be in the negative. Almost without exception, current accounts of the historical origins of Christianity are far too bland and innocuous to make intelligible either the devotion of early Christian martyrs or the hostility of their murderers. Read commentaries on the Apocalypse and ask if they make clear why John was willing to go to jail? Read commentaries on Romans and ask if they would induce us to join in stoning Paul or in risking the thirty-nine lashes? Our own individual responses to the New Testament, as we listen to one chapter or another, will be authentic to the degree to which they make us aware of our own immediate involvement in the conflicts detailed by Paul in Rom 8:38, 39 or by John in Rev 11:19-14:5. In sum, when we become as conscious as was Paul of the futility of creation and of the freedoms won by Christ, we will be able to understand apocalyptic visions and the powerful loyalties and vindictive enmities they released.

8 A VISION OF THE DEATH OF DEATH

(Revelation 19:11–21:4)

In Paul's list of things that contribute to the futility of all creation, he puts "life and death" first. Of this pair, death is the more obvious culprit, inasmuch as it proves that no living creature is exempt from the "bondage to decay." This compelled people to take notice how Christianity dealt with the chain of martyrs-and-murderers which had begun with Abel and Cain, and with the ravages of mortality which had begun with Adam and Eve. It is clear that Christian thinking about these casualties of the war in heaven was shaped by apocalyptic traditions of which John's visions were representative. Perhaps the most fascinating of these visions is the one picturing the death of death. The vision may be divided into seven scenes, each having a different function.

The first of these scenes (19:11-16) pictures Jesus Christ in his role as commander of the armies of heaven.

> ● One guideline is No. 12: an interpreter of apocalyptic prophecy must be adept in grasping the poetic and symbolic nuances in the prophet's language.

I saw heaven opened. This phrase informs us immediately that John is dealing with the realm of the invisible and that he intends to convey a vivid impression of that realm, precisely as in earlier visions (4:1; 11:19; 15:5). The prophet has adopted conventions that go back as far as Ezekiel (Ezek 1:1). Thus he warns readers that everything that follows, including the term *death*, is part and parcel of the vision. All is symbolic and nothing representational.

This applies of course to the rider on the *white horse* which makes *war*. (cf. Rev 6:2; Zech 1:8; 6:3, 6). Unlike other warriors, this commander exercizes the power of purity (*white*) and defeats his enemies by judging them *in righteousness* (Rev 6:10; 11:18; 16:5; Ps 96:13; Isa 11:4). He is qualified to judge those enemies because his life has become the perfect standard of *faithfulness* and *truth* (Rev 1:5; 3:14; 17:14; 21:5; 22:6). *Like a flame of fire* his eyes penetrate the inmost secrets of every heart and overcome all efforts at deception (1:14; 2:18; 5:6). The *diadems* on his head qualify him to defeat the dragon and its puppet-beasts, whose diadems (symbols of royal sovereignty) have proved to be so impressive that people are led to suppose that no one can fight against the dragon (Rev 4:4; 9:7; 12:3; 13:1; 14:14). No one knows the *name* of this horseman (since knowledge of the name signifies power to command the one named, Rev 2:17; 3:12; 14:1; 15:4; 22:4); yet that name is *The Word of God*, i.e., God's way of speaking to his people (John 1:1, 14). That name also makes him the *King* over all other kings (Rev 1:5; 17:14, 18; 20:4, 6; 22:5; Deut 10:17; Dan 2:47). Each symbol points to the work of Christ as spokesman for God and as leader of *the armies of heaven*, those who follow their leader, dressed in white linen and riding white horses (3:5, 18; 4:4; 6:11; 7:9, 13; 14:4, 13). The key to the whiteness of both linen and horses is to be found in the phrase "clad in a robe dipped in blood." In John's poetry this paradox of white robes dipped in red blood points unmistakably to the purity revealed in Jesus' death for others. In short, John's thinking about death is controlled by Jesus' death in its vicarious and redemptive aspect.

In the second scene (19:17-21) John describes in greater detail the war in heaven between this king of kings and the armies of all those kings arrayed against him.

> ● The vision illustrates our third guideline: an interpreter needs to be alive to the conflicts with both visible and invisible foes produced by the distinctive vocation of the prophets and their communities.

The symbolic language of the previous scene persists. Three specific symbols are decisive, in that the meanings that are assigned to them by the interpreter determine the accuracy of interpretation. First of all, the *sword* used by this commander issues *from his mouth* (Rev 1:16; 2:12, 16; Isa 49:2); this image corresponds to the earlier name, *The Word of God*. The death of his enemies is the result of using this sword! The *rod of iron* signifies that kind of power which enables the king of kings to rule the nations (Rev 2:27; 12:5; Ps 2:9). The power is real, but it is a special kind of power that must be consistent with that sword, that Word. Then there is the symbol of the *wine press*, pointing to God's final judgment, which again must remain consistent to the other symbols in the vision (Rev 14:20; 16:19; 17:2; 18:3; Isa 63:3; Lam 1:15; Joel 3:13; cf. the modern "battle hymn": "He is trampling out the vintage where the grapes of wrath are stored").

The armies involved are undoubtedly real, but they are not to be hastily made equivalent to specific historical nations, since they are heavenly armies, identified only by their commanders: Jesus with his robe dipped in blood, versus the kings of the earth, the earth-beast and the sea-beast, here spoken of as the false prophet. The details are gory enough to distract the attention of squeamish readers; yet the clues to the central meanings are clear enough. Exegesis must recognize these clues. The *only* force utilized by the rider on the white horse is the sword of his mouth. The *only* source of power for his opponents is their ability to deceive their armies. The primary form of action taken by those armies is that of worshiping the beast. Death is used by both commanders to give effect to their power, though the deaths that they inflict become quite different kinds of death. John may have intended the picture of "the great supper of God" as a gruesome parody of the Christian Eucharist. Whether or not that is the case, this battle scene brings to a vivid climax the invisible warfare between these two armies, a climax that underscores the terrible fate of all who are deceived by the demonic trinity.

So we move to the third scene (20:1-3), which marks a further step in God's judgment.

> • In the previous scene the prophet had dealt with the war against the more immediate enemies of God's people: sea-beast, earth-beast, false prophet, kings of the earth. Now he turns to the ultimate enemy, which in chap. 12 had been given three alternate titles: the dragon, the devil, Satan. Consequently in this scene, Guideline 4 comes into play, which obliges interpreters to respect the connections which the prophet has seen between the vocation of God's people and the ultimate war between God and Satan.

Satan is identified as the ultimate source of deception. When that deception is overcome, he is locked into the bottomless pit. That action marks the beginning of the millennium, the thousand years. So the scene impels readers to ask who it is who overcomes this power to deceive and how their action initiates this period of a thousand years. Or, another form of the same question, How and when is Satan's power to bind replaced by the power to bind Satan?

The answer is given in the fourth scene (20:4-6), which perhaps provides a more precise date for the beginning of the millennium. Here Satan's binding is made to coincide with the resurrection of "the souls of those who had been beheaded for their testimony to Jesus and for the word of God" (cf. 19:13). In an earlier vision John had shown that Satan's use of death to defeat Jesus had boomeranged because Jesus used the same death to defeat Satan. John now sees the same reversal operating in the murders of the martyrs. They too were using the sword that was the Word of God to destroy Satan's power to deceive. He came under their power at the very moment he used his power over them. Their death had represented "the confrontation of the power of death with the Word of God."[1] As victors in that confrontation they began to reign with Christ, immune to the ravages of the second death. "This death is glorious with the glory of another world, the real world of God."[2]

> ● Accordingly, Guideline 5 becomes applicable: an expert interpreter will develop an empathy for visions that link the vocation of God's people to ultimate beginnings (the authority of sin and death over Adam, Eve, and their descendants) and to ultimate endings (a victory over sin and death, and bondage to Satan's wiles).

In describing the beginning of the millennium, the prophet uses language that is native to apocalyptic tradition but language that to modern ears is too bizarre and fanciful to be persuasive. It may be helpful simply to focus attention upon the issues that are present wherever early Christians were beheaded because of their testimony to Jesus (v 4). No one at

[1]Stringfellow, *An Ethic for Christians and Other Aliens in a Strange Land*, p. 141.
[2]S. Moore, *The Crucified Jesus Is No Stranger* (New York: Seabury, 1977), p. 64.

that time (or later) could avoid asking: in that death, who was really the winner and who was the loser? If the Christian lost, his enemies won. If the Christian won, his enemies lost. One must choose between these two options. And judging by visible measurements of the situation, only the first option would have seemed to be true. But to the prophet, God revealed in the vision of the thrones in heaven (v 4) the truth of the other option. Furthermore, the interpreter must deal with the possibility that in the case of this particular death more was at stake than the fate of these specific individuals and their personal enemies. What if *this* death represented the history-long struggle between good and evil, "right forever on the scaffold, wrong forever on the throne"? What if *this* death represented the continuing vocation of God's people and the continuing rejection of that vocation? What if this event was a climactic incident in the long warfare between God and Satan? If this death represented the bondage to death of all creation? In this case the vision of the victorious rider on the white horse would convey to the prophet the assurance from God of an unprecedented defeat of Satan by all who shared "in the first resurrection." It was in fact that defeat that marked the beginning of the millennium.

The fifth scene (20:7-10) describes the ending of the millennium, when Satan is released from the abyss. We must ask how that release functions in the message of the prophet to his readers, who, of course, had not yet fulfilled their vocation. For one thing, this release coincides with a renewal of Satan's power to deceive. The martyrs had overcome this power, but not so Gog and Magog, the nations at the four corners of the earth. Deceived by Satan, these nations gather for a final battle against the camp of the saints.

● This mysterious figure of speech, Gog and Magog, comes from an earlier prophet, Ezek 38-39. By applying Guideline 11, an exegete can compare John's version with Ezekiel's and

discover how John has adapted Scripture to serve a new
function. The idea of a millennium may have had its source
here.

There is another contrast between the beginning and
the ending. The beginning had been marked by the power of
the first resurrection—the victory won by the Messiah and
the martyrs. The ending will be marked by the victory of the
beloved city over the massed hostility of the nations. That
city must demonstrate its communal power to defeat the
demonic trinity of forces: the false prophet, the beast from
the sea, and the great Serpent that had invaded Eden and
succeeded in getting humanity banned from Paradise. It is
the victory of this city over all historical enemies that is
celebrated by the banishment of this trinity into the lake of
fire. The idea of the millennium is a picturesque way of
connecting the first with the final victory and also
distinguishing them.

● Here readers are reminded of the relevance of Guideline
14. Interpreters must avoid transposing heavenly visions into
human measurements of months and years. In every
generation there are exegetes who believe they can date on
human calendars the beginning and the end of the
millennium. And almost always an exegete can persuade a
small clientele of the accuracy of those dates. But the result
always aborts the message of John. It denies his concern for
his own congregations and the emergencies they were facing.
It empties of ultimate significance the victories which the
martyrs had already won over Satan. It replaces the dynamics
of deception and moral struggle with the manipulation of
dates and numbers. It distracts the attention of the church
from its real enemies and its ultimate choices.

The sixth scene (20:11-15) reminds us that the end of the
warfare with Satan was not sufficient for John. Together with

his readers he faced a reality even more ultimate than Satan.
The final enemy is "Death and Hades." Inasmuch as the
experience of death is universal, death is here viewed as an
essential feature of the first heaven and earth. If Death and
Hades are to lose their power, this heaven and earth must
"flee away." No place must remain for them, and they must
yield up all those mortals whom they hold captive. Death
itself must die. Hades must cease to be a prison.

So John saw a great white throne. And enthroned was One
who wielded authority not alone over the ancient Serpent
but over that heaven and earth, over that sea which is the
slimy headquarters of Satan, and over Death and Hades and
all their hostages. The symbol of this authority—the books.
There are books in which is written God's judgment of the
dead, and there is the book of life with the names of all who
share God's life, victors forever over the power of Hades.[3]

Because the prophet John turned visions into words, great
artists who turn words back into pictures are often of major
help to interpreters. Among these painters we should
include Michelangelo, and among his paintings we should
include the fresco of the Last Judgment, which is located on
the wall above the altar in the Sistine Chapel in Rome. Here
we may find, in Leo Steinberg's words, "the world's greatest
artist, dedicating himself in his greatest work to what men
then conceived as their greatest concern."[4] "Three thousand
square feet of impending apocalypse" constitutes both the
artist's own "monumental confession of faith" and his way of
interpreting the prophecy: "Death and Hades gave up the

[3]In the interpretation of this symbol, the book of life, three points are
relevant. (1) John was using an image the meaning of which had been in part
defined by scripture (Exod 32:32; Ps 69:28; Dan 12:1). (2) The operative
word in the image is *life*, not *book*; accordingly one may find virtually the
same meaning in such other images as the tree of life and the water of life.
(3) The sharing in God's life is visualized in terms of the story of creation
before the intrusion of the serpent and death.

[4]*Daedalus*, 109 (1980): 207, 209.

dead in them" (Rev 20:13). One interesting aspect of that interpretation is the way in which the artist expressed his own personal relationship to the victory of Christ. Steinberg shows that in order to do this Michelangelo constructed his painting along a significant axis that connected the Prince of Hell at the lower cornerstone to the risen Christ at the upper keystone. On that axis, the artist included his own self-portrait at a point where the descending line to the lower cornerstone expressed his own "consciousness of demerit." But the same portrait is also located on the ascending line, which links the artist to the keystone wound in Christ's side and to the crown of thorns, thus expressing his Christian hope (pp. 236-38). Another interesting aspect of the fresco is its unconventional way of picturing Christ's success in freeing the dead from their prisonhouse. By his death Christ harrowed hell and secured humanity's redemption from death itself. Furthermore, by placing this "confession of faith" and this way of reading Revelation 20 immediately above the Sistine altar, the artist succeeded in "dramatizing the inmost sense of the altar" as the place where death's tyranny has been broken.[5] In all this, Michelangelo comes closer to the symbolic language of the prophet than do many modern evangelists who exploit each sign that the end of the world is at hand.

Another effective translation of this symbolism may be found in the Requiem Mass:

> The trumpet, sending its wondrous sound
> throughout the tombs of every land,
> will gather all before the throne.

> Death and nature will be astounded
> when all creation rises again
> to answer to the Judge.

[5]Ibid., p. 250.

A written book will be brought forth,
    in which everything will be contained
    by which the world will be judged.

And when the Judge takes his place,
    whatever is hidden will be made manifest;
    nothing will remain unpunished.[6]

The seventh and final scene (21:1-4) shows that John was not satisfied simply with describing the negation of the negative (the death of Death). Christ's message about a realm where death shall be no more (21:4) was important, but more important were positive descriptions of the life with God. This climactic scene unfolds in three steps—two visions and one audition. *"I saw"*: a new heaven and a new earth, wholly separate from the first creation. Here there is no sea (the source of all rebellion against the Creator). *"I saw"*: within that new creation a new city, from which all frustration, all corruption, all division had been removed. *"I heard . . . from the throne"*: this word is the climax. All that has transpired earlier is prologue to this word: And the key announcement is this: "the dwelling of God is with men." The banishment of Satan, the death of Death, the creating of a new heaven and earth—these open the way for God's presence in this city, seen as the highest good and the ultimate promise. Where he is, there death cannot rule. Where Death is dead, there can be no suffering and no mourning. To live as his people in his presence is the greatest source of strength, the substance of worship and the experience of the new creation. To inherit this city is John's perception of what is at stake in the warfare between Christ's army and its adversaries. The *apocalypsis* (revelation) conveyed by this vision as a whole (its seven scenes) is God's pledge of his eternal presence in this city.

[6]This version from Verdi, *Requiem*.

- To do justice to such a text, interpreters will need to apply, at least in their imagination, the second Guideline: they will need to become members of that community whose vocation is defined by the purpose and the presence of that holy city.

Before concluding this chapter let us comment on the relation between the millennium and the various meanings assigned by John to the word *death*. Death is used as a weapon of Satan in deceiving people with regard to his possession of final power; that kind of death ends when the deceit ends, when that power is terminated. So death is what happens when people are deceived and sin against the truth. By contrast, Christ uses death as a weapon to overcome those deceits and to demonstrate the power of vicarious and redemptive love. Accordingly the same event that Satan used to exhibit his power becomes an event in which that power is made useless. Because death comes to all people, imprisoning all the dead in Hades, both Death and Hades continue to rule as long as the first heaven and earth continue. Their rule is symbol of the futility and bondage that have characterized that creation since the sin of Adam and Eve. But with the creation of a new heaven and earth that futility and bondage are terminated. The death of Death becomes a sure sign of God's presence with his people. The imaginative richness of this language preserves the reality of death, insists upon its universality, but at the same time recognizes its mysterious aspects. Most of all, John was concerned with the many different ways in which death is an inevitable companion of the vocation of the church, and in which the death of Death is an expression of the fulfillment of that vocation.

9 THE DISCERNMENT OF VICTORY OVER DEATH

(Hebrews 2:1–4:13)

In shifting attention from Apocalypse to Epistle, we move from visions to sermons. Those sermons, as we shall see, reflect an ability to see the invisible, on the part of both preacher and congregation. We move also from the heavenly habitat of the dragon to the earthly habitat of those "made a little lower than the angels." We move from the gift of prophecy to other gifts, among which the gift of discernment will come into focus. In short, we will notice differences between the two documents, although behind the differences we will see a similar cluster of convictions about that victory over death that has been won in heaven.

The preacher reminds his congregation of their immediate past. Their salvation "was declared at first by the Lord [Jesus as a prophet], and it was attested to us by those who heard him [the apostles as prophets], while God also bore witness by signs and wonders and various miracles and by gifts of the Holy Spirit distributed according to his own will [including the gifts of understanding the prophetic messages]" (2:3, 4). Thus the preacher distinguished three stages in the story of salvation, each stage marked by the activity of the Holy Spirit, which itself became God's own witness to the decisive change in human affairs.

This retrospect was important; even more important, however, was the conception of worship in which preacher and congregation were immediately engaged. The congregation must be made aware that at that very place, in that very moment, their Lord was present among them for the purpose of speaking to them. First, he addressed God with words from Ps 22:22:

> I will proclaim your name to my brethren,
> in the midst of the congregation I will praise you.
> (Heb 2:12; my own translation)

In this bold reinterpretation of the Psalm, the risen Lord speaks in the first person singular. He speaks to his kinfolk about God, and to God for the congregation. By this double act of proclamation and praise, this living mediator continues his prophetic work, although in this case through the mouth of a preacher who in a quite literal way becomes his megaphone.

The same Lord continues to speak to the congregation, this time quoting Isa 8:17, 18:

> I will put my trust in him [God] . . .
> Here am I, and the children God has given me.

This quotation, in which the present Lord again identifies himself with the Scriptural "I", expresses several important convictions. In the mouth of the risen Jesus, it indicates what trust in God really means, thus including the congregation in the action of yielding such trust to God. The quotation identifies those worshipers as gifts that God had given to Jesus, and it accents their solidarity as a single entity. Three basic convictions can alone explain these innovative scriptural quotations: the role of Jesus as a living revealer, the role of the preacher as spokesman for the risen Lord, the role of the worshipers as children given to Jesus.

● The literary form of these texts strengthens the suggestion that this preacher was himself consciously speaking as a prophet and that the congregation would consciously react to his words as to the words of a prophet. The use of the personal pronoun "I" is very similar to John's use of the same pronoun in his vision (Rev 1:17–3:22). The suggestion is supported by a similar appeal in Heb 3:7 for worshipers to listen to what the Holy Spirit is saying. These comments strengthen David Hill's belief that this preacher did, indeed, fill the role of prophet.[1]

The preacher's sermon also made significant use of another passage from Scripture, Psalm 8, reinterpreting it in the light of the salvation that Jesus had won. Jesus was no other than "the Son of man" whom God had made "lower than the angels" and had crowned "with glory and honor" (2:7). But the preacher was not content with assertion only; he needed to explain the link between Jesus' story and the Psalm. He had become lower than the angels by way of his suffering, a suffering of death, by which he had himself been made perfect and had been able to sanctify his brothers and sisters. That suffering had been the way by which God had crowned Jesus with glory and honor, so that everything had been put in subjection to him. As fully as in John's apocalypse, the story of Jesus' passion dominates this sermon.

But the sermon had to make clear the bond that united the story of Jesus to the story of this congregation. The death of Jesus had been a "death for every one" (2:9). Because all were included in his death, his glorification also contained a promise of glory for everyone.

[1]*New Testament Prophecy*, pp. 141 ff.

• As I read this passage, I see the preacher reading the text in such a way as to distinguish *man* from the *Son of man*. Originally the Psalmist had seen these two as identical; the preacher in Hebrews, however, had adopted the Christian identification of the Son of man with Jesus. Accordingly he can witness to the subjection of all things to the *Son of man*, recognizing, of course, that such subjection to *man* cannot yet be seen. Accordingly, his exegesis of Psalm 8 centers on the distinctive suffering of the *Son of man* as a way by which his solidarity with *man* (the whole Adamic community) is established.

Central to the sermon is the paradox that by being made lower than the angels, Jesus had received power over the angels. Angels have now become "ministering spirits" to serve "those who are to obtain salvation" (1:14). The suffering of death provides the same origin for Jesus and his kinfolk; the glory of the Son of man becomes the destiny of "many sons" (2:10). So, when the preacher announces the presence of this Son of man to the worshiping congregation, it is their inclusion within this origin, this destiny, and this family that is being proclaimed.

But why, we must ask, did the preacher feel that this revelation was needed? The answer is this: each of his sermons was a "word of exhortation." This was a typical aspect of the role of each prophet, to provide pastoral guidance for the needs of the moment. In this case, those needs seem to be defined in terms of specific temptations that had come to a focus in fears of death (2:14-15). The logical structure underlying his effort to counter these temptations must be recovered in the following assertions:

—God's greatest enemy is the devil, who is therefore also the ultimate enemy of both the Son of man and man.

—The devil wields the power of death over all those who share in flesh and blood.

—That power of the devil is clinched by the fear of death
   on the part of all men.
—The defeat of the devil requires that men be freed from
   this fear, so that death ceases to be the instrument of
   bondage and becomes the instrument of freedom.
—Such freedom has been accomplished by the Son of
   man. In faithfulness to God's appointment he became
   flesh and blood, suffered the attacks of the devil, was
   tempted by the fear of death, but, in repelling that
   temptation, became worthy of glory.
—God's design and Jesus' faithfulness to it had been
   motivated by the desire to free "the sons of Abraham"
   and to expiate their sins.
—Those sons and those sinners were immediately
   represented by the congregation's hearing or reading
   this sermon. They had received through Jesus "a
   heavenly call" (2:3, 4; 3:1-2). In recent weeks they had
   been tempted by their exposure to public abuse, but
   they had become reconciled to the plundering of their
   possessions (10:32-34).
—This congregation was again being tempted by the power
   of the devil through the fear of death. Fresh persecution
   carried with it the prospect of bloodshed (12:4).
—Accordingly, the Holy Spirit was warning them that in
   this new period of wilderness testing, their hearts could
   be hardened by the deceitfulness of sin (3:13) or they
   could prove themselves "God's house" by holding fast
   their confidence and pride "in our hope" (3:6).
That is the world of assumptions and convictions that
provides the context for this exhortation of the preacher:

Since therefore the children share in flesh and blood, he
himself likewise partook of the same nature, that through
death he might destroy him who has the power of death, that
is, the devil, and deliver all those who through fear of death

were subject to lifelong bondage. For surely it is not with angels that he is concerned but with the descendants of Abraham. Therefore he had to be made like his brethren in every respect, so that he might become a merciful and faithful high priest in the service of God, to make expiation for the sins of the people. For because he himself has suffered and been tempted, he is able to help those who are tempted (2:14-18).

When we ponder the nuances of that exhortation within the context of the convictions outlined above, we may be able to be more specific about the gift of discernment which the Holy Spirit would provide for this congregation as it responded to the preacher. Their obedience to this exhortation would presuppose their discernment of the presence in their midst of the risen Lord, their discernment of the presence as well of the devil, hiding in their secret fear of death, their discernment of their sin of fear and the bondage concealed in that fear, their discernment of the expiation of that sin by their high priest. They were summoned by their preacher, in fact, to *see* Jesus, the apostle and high priest of their confession (3:1) and in seeing him to become conscious of the presence of "God's house." Such a vision, such consciousness would take the form of rejecting the devil's lure, by way of stubborn pride in their hope. All this is precisely what their "heavenly call" entailed.

One of the greatest preachers of all time, Augustine, had pondered long the message of Revelation and of Hebrews concerning the conflict between Christ and Satan. He developed what has been called the mousetrap theory: "The devil exulted when Christ died, but by this very death of Christ the devil was vanquished, as if he had swallowed the bait in the mousetrap. He rejoiced in Christ's death, like a bailiff of death. What he rejoiced in was then his own undoing. The cross of the Lord was the devil's mousetrap;

the bait by which he was caught was the Lord's death."[2]
Much the same line of thought lies behind 1 Cor 2:8.

• The imagery used in Hebrews has made it very easy for
interpreters to miss the thrust of the appeal. The termi-
nology—temptation, sin, expiation, priesthood—invites
readers to think of another context: a temple, an altar,
prayers, sacrifices, rituals, vestments, priests. It takes a
revolution in the readers' imagination to define *this*
temptation and sin in terms of the fears of death, and *this*
expiation in terms of Jesus' victory over these fears, and *this*
priesthood in terms of the sharing of that victory with a
company of real or potential martyrs. From the beginning it
has required the gift of the Holy Spirit for listeners and
readers to grasp the force of the preacher's words.

The foregoing analysis of this sermon should indicate why
charismatic gifts were needed to understand what the Holy
Spirit was saying, a gift to the preacher and a twin gift of
discernment on the part of his listeners, both gifts
inseparable from that common vocation which emerged
from the Passion story of Jesus. By his call he had established
with them a common origin and destiny. His call had
removed them so far from the range of ordinary human
existence as to require a unique degree of disciplined
imagination if his followers were to remain residents of
"God's house."

The same analysis should also reveal basic congenialities
between the sermons in the book of Hebrews and the visions
of John in Revelation. Each of the basic convictions outlined
above, which indicate the mind-set of the preacher, can be
paralleled in John's thought-world, and especially in his
vision of the death of Death. For both, Satan is God's
primary antagonist, and death clinches Satan's hold over

[2]Sermon 263, translated by M. Schapiro.

humanity. For both it is the fear of death that reinforces Satan's sovereignty, and for both that role of death is terminated by the victory won by Jesus and by members of his armies who demonstrate his courage. For many readers, however, John's picture of the millennium provides such a sharp contrast that other similarities between the two prophets are given little weight. It is true that the preacher does not use the same scriptural texts as John to indicate this period of a thousand years between the imprisonment of Satan and his later release. Yet when we grasp the function of this period of bondage in the Apocalypse we can discover a similarity of function in Hebrews. This preacher also distinguishes the first victory over Satan from the final victory when all enemies will be subjected to *man*. For both prophets, that first victory provides the essential memory to generate the confidence that is needed; that final victory reminds them of the sober courage they will need to face the more subtle and more sustained attack still to come from the demonic hordes. For both prophets, the present period of the church is a time when maximum alertness is needed, and for both that period is short.

● This comparison of the two prophets leads me to observe that many modern readers place too much weight upon John's conception of the millennium. The fact that Hebrews conveyed essentially the same message without recourse to a millennium indicates that the latter concept is not essential to faith in Christ's victory over death.

Similarities in thought between the two prophets make it desirable to use each to enhance our understanding of the other. Here we must be content to suggest a single set of contributions. If we were to move from Hebrews to Revelation and from the sermon on the Son of man to the vision of the millennium, we would more easily recognize the psychic and moral implications of John's vision. No less than the preacher was the prophet seeking to penetrate the secret fears of death on the part of his readers. In both cases those fears were precipitated by historical conflicts in which powerful human institutions were exercising mastery over the life and death of Christians. Accordingly, the psychic dread was inseparable from moral decisions which determined the survival of both members and churches. When we recognize these factors as conditioning John's image of the millennium, we are less likely to get lost in mythological magnitudes, less likely to correlate that image of a thousand years with some span on a historical timeline, less likely to change our view of John himself from a responsible leader of churches to a crystal-ball futurologist.

So, too, if we move from Revelation to Hebrews, and from vision to exhortation, we will more readily recognize the mythological range and depth lying behind the preacher's sermon. With that recognition will come a fuller appreciation of the degree to which the moral exhortation is grounded in universal forces that operate in all cultures and generations. Simultaneously, we will be less likely to think of the preacher as an "establishment figure," an apologist for the priesthood, whose horizon of concern is provided by ecclesiastical ritual, by the institutional means for the expiation of sins, by the internal life of a religious community. His concern with the victory over the fear of death, made accessible by the Son of man, is so cosmic in scope as to require a fully mythological context.

10 A VISION OF THE HOLY CITY
(Revelation 21:9–22:9)

None of John's visions is quoted more widely than this, and many perverse interpretations reflect its popularity. For instance, because it often appears in funeral liturgies, it is often assumed to be God's assurance of life after death for all individuals, without respect for their life before death. Such a use was very far from John's original intent. His concern was the present reality of the holy city, the very particular bride of this very particular Lamb. Thus his vision was much more relevant to the life of believers before death than to their life after death. If life after death entered the circle of his awareness, it was the life of this community after the death of the Lamb rather than after the deaths of his followers.

A second common perversion springs from popular affections for the artistic beauty of John's picture of the holy city, affections which often reduce the vision to a sentimental effusion that stifles rather than stimulates the desire to cope with John's thought. Such sentimentality encourages readers to ignore the stern threats of exclusion from the city (21:8, 27; 22:3, 15). In fact, several churches, in adopting this text for their lectionaries, have quietly deleted those threats, a dubious index of their respect for John's authority. Such distaste for John's realism makes the use of this "beautiful poem" the occasion for an ego trip for pious souls whose "belief in a future life is . . . a barrier to honest religion because it shows the greed and self-interest that a religious faith ought to destroy."[1]

Group egoism leads a religious community to interpret John's vision as a divine corroboration of its own holiness and will-to-power. To be sure, John's vision seems to support this reading, for it presents the descent from heaven of a holy city; but it is a city and not a church. It would defeat his purpose to make the boundaries of that city coincide with any particular historical embodiment of religion. His city is but one aspect of a new heaven and a new earth, a mystery of which we could say both "never here" and "ever here." To see that city, John needed the help of an angel and the Spirit. To discern the relevance of his message, interpreters need similar help. If we are to bend our reactions to conform to the contour of his thought, we need to examine carefully the details of the vision.

Three essential features appear in the opening paragraph (21:9-14). First of all, the existence of this city is traced directly to supernatural action. It comes down from God and is filled with his glory; in both of these respects there is an implicit antithesis to the tower of Babel. Because the city is God's gift of a Bride for the Lamb, the origins are to be traced to the self-sacrifice of that Lamb, with implicit reference to the Passover sacrifice that recalled the Exodus from Egyptian captivity. In the second place, the city is surrounded by "a great high wall," that provides full security to its residents and firm exclusion to its enemies (cf. Isa 60:18). There is logic in the fact that John is introduced to the city by the same angel which had poured out the seven bowls of wrath on the great harlot (antithesis to the bride) and on the city of Babylon (antithesis to the new Jerusalem) (21:9; 17:1 ff.). "Travesty

---

[1]Brenan, *Thoughts in a Dry Season*, p. 51.

and reality . . . plague and blessing, are two sides of one coin throughout Revelation."[2] Finally, the holy city is presented as a fulfillment of God's promise to a specific historical community. It is not anonymous, but bears the name Jerusalem. Its gates bear the names of the twelve tribes; its foundations bear the names of the twelve apostles of the Lamb. Patriarchs, apostles, Lamb—these are definitive. Their several stories coalesce in a single story, the story of the city. In the calling of the city God's separate callings of these leaders are consummated. A measure of the continuity is the fact that John's vision has been shaped by the earlier version of Ezekiel (48:30-35). In both visions, the meaning of the city is provided by the simple phrase "the Lord is there."

Further important features of the holy city are specified in the second paragraph (21:15-21). Here the continuity with the past is balanced by discontinuity, radical immanence by equally radical transcendence. The dimensions of this city can be measured only by a rod of gold given to the prophet by the angel (11:1; 21:15). This rod was both a human instrument (a prophet used it) and an angelic instrument (an angel gave it). The extent of the city, as measured by this rod, far exceeds the human imagination. The symbolic number twelve thousand can be translated into the nonsymbolic distance of fifteen hundred miles. But consider this dimension: the city is in the form of a cube: it has a height of fifteen hundred miles! The cube was "a natural symbol of perfection."[3] A city that reaches so far as this in every direction is a city in which no one has ever lived. A city of such proportions reduces to nonsense all efforts by interpreters to gauge its distance in calendar years from some point in human history, whether A.D. 70 or 1982.

Another index of transcendence is the description of its walls as jasper, its streets as gold, its foundations as precious

[2]Sweet, *Revelation*, pp. 302-3.
[3]Ibid., p. 305.

jewels.[4] Perhaps the hyperbole reaches its highest point in
the notation that each of the twelve gates had been carved
out of a single pearl. The gates marked entrances through a
wall measuring 144 cubits (whether breadth or height is not
specified). What pearl can be this large? What gate this
small? The hyperbole is so unimaginable as to be humorous, and yet a serious intent is hidden in the humor. How
can one measure in spatial terms the point where a community encounters God's glory? How much space is needed
to mark the conjunction between the temporal and the
eternal? How does God's glory expand the size of a pearl?
How does a share in his city reduce the size of the gate? The
prophet was in contact with two incommensurables, both
real and both to be seen in their relation to each other. Each
gate into this city is carved out of a single pearl.[5] So in the
first paragraph of John's vision we have detected the desire
to emphasize the continuity of the city with God's calling to
patriarchs and apostles, and in the second paragraph the
desire to stress a glory that transcended every historical
embodiment. Accordingly we conclude that the holiness of

[4]The prophet seems to have felt that such extravagance is required to do
justice to the glory of God. His vision is "the description of the indescribable
in unforgettable terms," one of the definitions of great poetry. Because of
his adept use of extreme hyperbole, no historical city can serve as the model
for this painting.

[5]It is the meeting of incommensurables of this order that prompted Emily
Dickinson's verse:

> Heaven is so far of the mind
> That were the mind dissolved,
> The site of it by architect
> Could not again be proved.
>
> 'Tis vast as our capacity,
> As fair as our idea,
> To him of adequate desire
> No further 'tis than Here.

The Complete Poems of Emily Dickinson (Boston: Little, Brown, 1930),
pp. 330-31.

this city constitutes the source of the holiness of God's people, while the historical existence of that people always points beyond and above itself to a holiness not its own.

Now in the third paragraph (21:22-27) the vision appears to convey even more inclusive connotations. We notice in particular three symbolic statements. First of all, there is no temple in the city. This seems to suggest that its descent from heaven marks the obsolescence of religious institutions, all the while it marks the fulfillment of their basic function. Second, the city has no need for sun or moon. Night as a symbol of blindness, lostness, darkness, and death has been replaced by the day of the Lord, with its corresponding symbolic richness. That day is the new creation of Day One, when God had created light, the light of his presence (see above, chap. 3). Third, all kings and nations bring their glory into this city. Thus the vision declares the relevance of the city to all social and political institutions, from all times and places. The function of the city is to provide their true fulfillment; their function is to contribute to its glory.

In his effort to do justice to the historical and cosmic dimensions of the city, however, the exegete must not overlook the role of the Lamb in that city. It is his throne that constitutes its center, its sovereignty. He *is* the temple. He *is* the lamp by which nations and kings walk. It is his book of life that determines exclusion and inclusion. He is Judge and Gatekeeper. In all these roles, of course, he shares the work of God Almighty. If political theology is involved in the vision, the Lamb is *the theo*-logian.

● Much attention is being given today to political theology, but without much use of the Apocalypse. And there are many commentaries on the Apocalypse which find in it very little by way of contribution to political ethics. William Stringfellow provides an exception to both rules in his book described among the Aids for the Interpreter at the end of this book.

He makes judicious and, on the whole, persuasive comments
on the relevance of the Apocalypse to current controversies
over governmental policies.

Few interpreters have surpassed the insight of Augustine:
"Two loves mark the origins of these two cities [Babylon and
Jerusalem]: self-love in contempt of God mark the earthly;
love of God in contempt of self mark the heavenly. The first
seeks the glory of men and the latter desires God only. . . .
One is led by the lust of sovereignty; in the other each person
serves the other in charity."[6]

Augustine appreciated the degree to which the role of the
Lamb transformed all ideas of holiness. Why is this city holy?
How did it become holy? How is its holiness to be
understood? The point of reference for answering all such
questions is the story of Jesus, "by your blood you ransomed
for God saints from every tribe . . . and you have made them
to be a kingdom" (5:9-10; my own translation). What
became of all other ideas of holiness in that story? Jesus was
arrested in a holy place and crucified as an enemy of the
temple. He aroused bitter opposition as one who did not
respect holy times, the Sabbaths, and the festivals. He
refused to observe rules about holy things, foods, dishes, and
so forth. By no means was Golgotha a holy place. His
execution was no holy rite. His sacrifice took place on an
altar that had never been sanctified by scripture or tradition.

Because it was through that death for others that he had
been made holy (sanctified) and had made others holy
(sanctified them as kings and priests), his successor prophets
came to define holiness by reference to his sufferings and
death. Places, times, rules, books, things—all these ceased
to be holy. Henceforth, holiness could be located only in
people and in human actions. His presence made the city
holy. He shared his holiness with the "armies dressed in

[6]*City of God,* XII, 16.

white," but excluded from that holiness "anyone who practices abomination or falsehood" (21:27). It was such a definition of the holiness of this city that made John's vision entirely different from some innocuous exercise in aesthetic imagination.

So much is conveyed by these first paragraphs that a reader may well wonder what can be added in the remaining paragraphs. But two important components do appear. The first relates the holy city explicitly to the Genesis story of creation, to the tree of life growing on both sides of the river of the water of life. In these symbols the key word is life; the key conviction is faith that the end of all stories will bring to a full and rich completion their beginnings in the purposes of God.

The second component is the explicit identification of the residents of the holy city. The prophet has had his eye on these residents from the beginning. In fact, apart from their activity there would have been little purpose in the prophecy as a whole. The dominant image of the throne is made necessary by that activity: "his slaves shall worship him." This worship includes a collage of four elements:

> they shall see his face
> (the prophet's vision will become theirs)
> his name shall be on their foreheads
> (worship identifies them as his possession)
> the Lord God will be their light
> (he will guide all their walking)
> they shall reign forever
> (they will have power over demonic enemies)

Of course, to embrace all four of these elements, the usual conceptions of worship would need to be enlarged. Such enlargement might be suggested by substituting the word *worship* for *pain* in the following verses of Emily Dickinson:

> Pain expands the time,
> Ages coil within

The minute circumference
Of a single brain.

Pain contracts the time
Occupied with shot,
Gamuts of eternities
Are as they were not.[7]

Worship expands the time . . . contracts the time. The vision of worship before the throne of God and the Lamb functions in such a way as to do both. The Dickinson poem is relevant because the throne of the Lamb is inseparable from his pain.

In his next paragraph (22:6-9) the prophet brings into play a new dimension of his vision. Here we must notice the sequence of the angel's words, which are by no means anticlimactic. First comes a beatitude: "Blessed is the one who keeps the words of the prophecy of this book." The words are to be kept; in the idiom of the prophet, this means there is a command to be obeyed by the recipients of the address. Those who obey will receive the gift of the city. Then we read the staccato words of a command that shows what keeping the words really meant: "Worship God."

Neither the angel nor the prophet is to be worshiped. They are simply links in the chain of command: God, the Lamb, the angel, the prophet. When readers obey the command they, too, become links in the chain, colleagues of prophets and angels. So at the very end, the purpose of the whole prophecy comes clear: not to fuel the curiosity of readers about future events or to encourage gossip about heavenly secrets, not to add to the excitement over spiritual gifts or to guarantee a final lodging for God's favorites. Simply this command: worship God. Obedience to the command makes sense of the vision, as the vision makes sense of worship.

[7]*The Complete Poems of Emily Dickinson*, p. 336.

Here at the end John provides his own key to understanding the vision. Like other early Christian prophets he recognized that his vocation was designed to provide pastoral guidance—warnings, promises, exhortations, encouragements. None of his own visions of the coming of Christ drew him away from that assignment; rather they were viewed by him as a way of fulfilling that assignment. Worship had the potential of translating the vision into the life of the churches; conversely, the vision had the potential of translating worship into a language that disclosed its infinite reach and range.

- When we observe the climactic position of the command to worship God, this observation may suggest how we might think of the distance between the churches of Asia and the holy city, the new Jerusalem. One option, often followed, is to calculate that distance in months or years. This has the effect of separating the churches from Christ's coming by an impersonal, objective span of time. Another effect is to provide a false motivation for the command: "Because I am coming soon, get down on your knees!" Such an interpretation is quite wrong; it reduces the thought of both prophet and churches to sub-Christian levels. The command to worship indicates that there are other ways of measuring the decisive distance.

11 THE DISCERNMENT OF LIFE IN THE CITY
(Hebrews 12:1–13:25)

Now we turn to another homily in the Epistle to the Hebrews in which the preacher is primarily concerned with awakening the ability among his listeners to discern what the Spirit was saying to them. In this case the most important Guideline is No. 2: An interpreter must belong to a community that has been called into existence and given a distinctive vocation by that same God. In this sermon the most important verbs of command or exhortation are of two types: there are verbs calling for unusual perception—to look, to see, to listen, to consider; and there are verbs calling for symbolic action—to come, to go, to remember, to seek. Moreover, these two types of verbs are curiously interdependent. To see leads immediately to movement, while the movement itself is a form of vision. The duties of perception and of action are forms of life in the holy city, and only its questers can understand that interdependence. It is, in fact, the vocation and the objective of the preacher to arouse on the part of his hearers that kind of understanding. In this chapter, therefore, we wish to examine how this leader tried to provide that kind of pastoral guidance.

A first example is provided by the appeal to "look to" and to "consider" Jesus (12:1-4). Often we neglect to realize that this is a summons for each reader to have a vision, comparable to that of a prophet, a vision of Jesus "seated at the right hand of the throne of God." Moreover, the significance of this vision stemmed from memory of a specific story in which the cross and the joy were the central components. Vision and memory defined each other. Nor was this a vision of an isolated individual; Jesus was the central figure among a cloud of witnesses stretching at least from the sacrifice of Abel (11:4) to all the prophets (11:32). Faith took the form of seeing all the faithful, of being surrounded by them, and of obeying the obligations intrinsic to belonging in such a company.

What kinds of obligations were intrinsic to this vision and to this cumulative memory? Before answering, we recall that a chief obstacle to the prophetic vocation was the propensity to self-righteous hypocrisy and duplicity on the part of God's elect, a fact that requires the prophet to penetrate defensive masks and to destroy the facade of piety. The text at hand permits us to infer the character of "the sin which clings so closely": whatever leads runners not to "run with perseverance" this particular race . . . whatever induces weariness and faintheartedness . . . whatever leads them to fear disgrace rather than to despise it . . . dread of the hostility that is turned against these runners . . . dread of that discipline which involves pain and even bloodshed—all these are the targets of the preacher in this segment of his sermon. It takes little perspicuity to recognize that in most cases these sins remain secrets hidden in the hearts of sinners. The power of such temptations stems from the visible environment of the churches. Ability to counter that power with a still greater power requires an acute awareness of an invisible environment, nothing less than a charismatic vision of the throne of God. That vision must convey a vivid impression of the joy that is set before *them*.

In that first sample of the preacher's logic, the vision of

Jesus precedes the action demanded by it: looking to Jesus encourages his followers to endure hostility and persecution. In a second sample, the action appears to precede the vision: striving for peace enables the community to see the Lord. "Strive for peace with all men, and for the holiness without which no one will see the Lord" (v 14).

• At first sight this command seems to reflect a different social situation. Moreover, since this chapter is composed of diverse, axiomatic teachings, which perhaps circulated separately in the churches before this editor collected them, it may be unwise to link this command to the situation of persecution so prominent in vv 1-3. I am convinced, however, that this editor intended that very linkage. The two teachings are connected by the image of a father disciplining his sons by way of inducing the hostility of sinners (v 3). It had been by way of despising the shame of the cross (v 2) that Jesus had effectively defined his holiness (v 10). We conclude therefore that this command in v 14 illustrates how the action of obedience to this specific command enables a congregation to see the Lord, and how this vision provides the prospect as well as the retrospect for the community of disciples. When faith is defined by obedience to this command (v 14), Jesus becomes both its pioneer and the perfecter (v 2).

With that conclusion in mind, then, we ask what inferences may be drawn from this double command? For one thing, Christians have within reach a holiness that does in fact enable them to see God. For another, such holiness is to be defined, at least in part, by the activity of seeking peace in relations with all people, surely including the enemies who are threatening to shed their blood. For still another, this holiness and this peacemaking require strenuous and even dangerous activity. The preacher's command is precisely parallel to Jesus' beatitudes: "Blessed are the peacemakers . . . . Blessed are the pure in heart . . . . Blessed are those who are persecuted . . . . " In Matthew's sermon the use of synonymous parallelisms emphasizes the convergence of persecution, peacemaking, and purity of heart. In the sermon in Hebrews, we note a similar convergence of persecution, peace-seeking, and holiness. In both cases the vision of God is a promised consequence. Listeners in both cases are urged to perceive new connections: the vision of God is linked to the dangerous business of peace-seeking; holiness is defined not in terms of places or times or institutions or ceremonies, but in terms of actions vis-à-vis enemies and in terms of persons who are considered shameful by the general public. When we stop to think about this, we realize that such conceptions of holiness and of seeing God are the opposite of those normally adopted by Christian communitites. The preacher, like the prophet, seeks to penetrate the masks of self-righteousness behind which members of those communities live.

We turn now to examine still another vision that this preacher wanted his readers to experience. We must quote the entire text:

> You have come to Mount Zion and to the city of the living
> God, the heavenly Jerusalem, and to innumerable angels in
> festal gathering, and to the assembly of the first-born who are
> enrolled in heaven, and to a judge who is God of all, and to
> the spirits of just men made perfect, and to Jesus, the
> mediator of a new covenant, and to the sprinkled blood that
> speaks more graciously than the blood of Abel. See that you
> do not refuse him who is speaking. (12:22-25a).

I have left out the first word of this assertion: the word *but*. That lone word indicates that this mountain must be seen as different in decisive ways from Mt. Sinai. Sinai could be touched; this mountain is quite intangible. Unlike Sinai, this mountain does not threaten death to man or animal that touches it. The fears evoked by the two mountains are different; the covenants sealed on the two mountains are different. Listeners welcome the messages coming from Zion; they can endure these orders. Mount Zion is intangible; yet "you have come" to it. Here a voice speaks that can shake the earth.

What kind of audition is this? Whose voice is speaking? Discernment is clearly necessary. In verse 24 the speaker is identified as "the sprinkled blood." This voice speaks more graciously than the blood of Abel. This is surely because this is the blood of the new covenant. Both Jesus and Abel had been murdered, but only in one case did the murder become a channel of grace. Only in this case were members of the covenant community sprinkled with the blood of the mediator. This voice communicates grace. "Do not refuse him who is speaking." Who is this? Probably God who speaks through the sprinkled blood; through that blood the inaudible becomes audible for those with ears to hear.

It speaks graciously. Yes, but there is warning as well, a warning from heaven more ominous than any comparable warning from earth. The warning automatically applies to anyone who refuses to listen. Listeners must become aware that this God who speaks is a consuming fire (echoes of Sinai). The voice which is rejected (inaudible, of course) has the power to shake everything in creation that can be shaken. Normal earthquakes are mild in comparison.

In short, the description of this voice in its graciousness and in its ominousness is as good an example of prophetic hyperbole as John's image of the gates of pearl; both images are humorous and yet deadly serious. Preacher and prophet express the same positive command: "Let us offer to God acceptable worship" (12:28). Both warn in the strongest terms against that kind of rejection of God's words that would exclude believers from the city. Both define such worship and such rejection in radically new ways which require spiritual discernment to understand. Although they use slightly different images, both want their readers to sense the distance between the old and the new—in John's terms, the first heaven-and-earth versus the new heaven-and-earth; and in Hebrews' terms, the kingdom that cannot be shaken versus everything that can be and will be shaken.

There are differences, too, between the residents of the heavenly Jerusalem as seen by these two prophets; but the similarities are conspicuous. Both assume that the ultimate authority rests in the "judge who is God of all"; both visualize God speaking primarily through Jesus, a message of judgment and deliverance; both are aware of "the armies of heaven" as "the spirits of just men made perfect"; both attribute important roles to angels and to those powers in heaven who must be shaken out of their place (12:26). Most important of all, both prophets desire that their readers will become so keenly aware of their environment in the heavenly Jerusalem, by charismatic vision and/or audition, that their actions in their immediate social environments will constitute "acceptable worship" of this God who speaks to them from Mount Zion.

All this leads us to raise a question with regard to the preacher in Hebrews: What kinds of behavior does he wish to encourage among his readers that would manifest the presence of the "city of the living God"? Chap. 13 is filled with answers, from which we may select one or two.

● These are discussed as a way of applying Guideline No. 15: Realizing that future expectations are directly related to present behavior, an interpreter must relate prophetic visions to the horizons implicit in specific Christian experiences.

"Keep your life free from love of money, and be content with what you have; for he has said, 'I will never fail you nor forsake you.' Hence we can confidently say, 'The Lord is my helper, I will not be afraid; what can man do to me?' " (13:5, 6).

The assumptions are clear. The love of money and trust in God are mutually exclusive. Confidence in his care delivers a person from all fears of human enemies, including the fear of death. The hiddenness of temptation and the danger of self-deception are especially present in this case. So worshipers must listen to the voice of God, which comes to them through the *alter ego* of the preacher, quoting scripture but applying it in such a way as to provide contemporary dialogue between the worshipers and God, and allowing the community (we can confidently say) to support a command addressed to its individual members. To reject this command would be to reject congregation, preacher, and God. It would be to deny that the leader had spoken the word of God (v 7). The tacit context within which this command belongs is entirely similar to that of Paul in Romans 8 and of John in Revelation 2, 3.

> So Jesus suffered outside the gate in order to sanctify the people through his own blood. Therefore let us go forth to him outside the camp, and bear the abuse he endured. For here we have no lasting city, but we seek the city which is to come. Through him then let us continually offer up a sacrifice of praise to God, that is, the fruit of lips that acknowledge his name (13:12-15).

The name that is to be acknowledged is the name of one who endured abuse. Accordingly, this sacrifice of praise to God is made by those who go to him outside the camp and who bear the same abuse. Here is the altar; this is the high priest. Sharing his alienation from one city becomes the way of seeking another city. Worship is the way of seeking the city that is to come, but the way to worship is defined by Jesus' sacrifice for sin. Moreover the character of this city is etched sharply by the mode of seeking it. City, worship, Christ, suffering—these represent an essential quadrilateral so tightly bound together that no element can be rightly grasped without grasping all four. This thought continues in the following verse: "Do not neglect to do good and to share what you have, for such sacrifices are pleasing to God" (13:16). Here again is a definition of worship which determines the reverence and awe which the congregation is obliged to offer its God (12:28). It sounds like an innocuous truism, a pious moralism that really wields no clout in religious affairs. But the behavior that follows this innocent command is, in the thought-world of Hebrews, a way of fleeing from Babylon ("no lasting city") and of seeking the city that is to come. Obedience presupposes the giving of priority to the invisible and the inaudible realm earlier called Mount Zion. Such brotherly love is a way of recognizing that "our God is a consuming fire," whose voice shakes everything that can be shaken. It is a way of running the race with perseverance.

It is impossible to demonstrate in all these teachings that they are indeed transparent signs of earthly life that is oriented around the prophetic vision of the heavenly Jerusalem. But such orientation is clearly present in many of them. They embody a memory and a hope that presuppose ultimate beginnings and endings. Jesus stands at the beginning and at the end of their race as pioneer and perfecter of faith. The city to which they have come is also the city which they seek. The discipline that is manifested in their existence as sons points ahead to a share in the Father's holiness (12:10). Gratitude for receiving a kingdom that cannot be shaken prepares its heirs for the future shaking of earth and heaven (a distinction not unlike the millennium of Revelation 20). Each of their basic duties becomes a form of worship, in which Jesus has provided the paradigm of sanctuary, altar, priesthood, and sacrifice. Those readers who received the gift of discernment, the gift twin to the prophet's gift of vision, would have been fully able to understand the context within which every word in the benediction (13:20, 21) carried maximum meaning.

AIDS FOR THE INTERPRETER

All the basic biblical terms carry many special meanings, and apocalyptic language, in particular, imparts unusual symbolic nuances to many key words. It is therefore wise for every student to have at hand a dependable Bible dictionary, such as *The Interpreter's Dictionary of the Bible* (5 vols.) published by Abingdon Press (1962–76).

Students who are not content with the compact dictionary definitions and who will want to trace for themselves the biblical use of key apocalyptic symbols (e.g., thrones, trumpets) will find useful a concordance which lists all the passages using a specific symbol: Clinton Morrison, *An Analytical Concordance to the Revised Standard Version of the New Testament* (Philadelphia: Westminster, 1979).

For an introduction to the types of literary forms used by the apocalyptist, students may well consult Amos N. Wilder: *Early Christian Rhetoric: The Language of the Gospel* (Cambridge: Harvard University Press, 1971).

For a sample of how a student can, with the help of the Concordance, trace the aura of meanings conveyed by a given symbol (e.g., the clouds), reference may be made to my own *Christian Hope and the Second Coming* (Philadelphia: Westminster, 1954).

The more acquaintance one may develop with the history of apocalyptic thought in general, the more one will feel at home in dealing with examples in the New Testament. In this connection, the best collection of extra-biblical apocalyptic writings has been edited by Edgar Hennecke, *New Testament Apocrypha,* vol. 2, ed. Wilhelm Schneemelcher (Philadelphia: Westminster, 1965).

The most thorough analysis of the Old Testament origins of this pattern of thought is found in Paul D. Hanson, *The Dawn of Apocalyptic* (Philadelphia: Fortress, 1976).

A competent introduction to Jewish apocalyptic thought is available in David S. Russell, *The Method and Message of Jewish Apocalyptic* (Philadelphia: Westminster, 1964).

As we have seen, it is quite impossible to separate apocalyptic from prophecy in the early Christian church; accordingly books on the latter topic throw strong light on the former. This is true of two recent books: David Hill, *New Testament Prophecy* (Atlanta: John Knox, 1979) and Johannes Panagopoulos, ed., *Prophetic Vocation in the New Testament and Today* (Leiden: Brill, 1977).

Because the Book of Revelation is the major example of apocalyptic prophecy in the New Testament, commentaries on that book should be consulted. Of these there are many (George R. Beasley-Murray, Isbon Beckwith, Robert H. Charles, Austin M. Farrer, Wilfrid J. Harrington, Martin Kiddle, George E. Ladd, Leon Morris, Ronald H. Preston and Anthony T. Hanson). Of the many, two deserve special mention. In my judgment, the most thorough, dependable, and recent commentary is by George B. Caird, *The Revelation of St. John the Divine* (New York: Harper & Row, 1966). A more recent, imaginative commentary, designed for the general reader, has appeared in the Pelican series: John P. M. Sweet, *Revelation* (Philadelphia: Westminster, 1979).

My own book, *I Saw a New Earth* (Washington: Corpus Books, 1968), aims to guide a student's private study of the successive visions. It concentrates on the literary structures of those visions, and on the theological perspectives imbedded in them.

In chap. 6 of the current study we examined the message of Revelation chap. 12. Those who wish to extend that study are referred to Adela Yarbro Collins, *The Combat Myth in the Book of Revelation* (Chico, Cal.: Scholar's Press, 1976).

In chaps. 8 and 10 we examined the closing visions in Revelation. An extension of that study may be found in Matthias Rissi, *The Future of the World* (London: SCM Press, and Naperville, Ill.: Allenson Books, Studies in Biblical Theology, vol. 23).

Throughout Christian history, artists, fascinated by the Apocalypse, have been among its most stimulating interpreters. Among visual artists, every student should consult the famous woodcuts of Albrecht Dürer, *The Apocalypse*. Among poets, few interpretations have been as influential as John Milton's in *Paradise Lost*. Novelists have often surpassed exegetes in their interest in and penetration of apocalyptic symbolism. Students who wish to pursue this line of study may well begin with John R. May, *Toward a New Earth: Apocalypse in the American Novel* (University of Notre Dame Press, 1972).

Composers also have proved to be able expositors. Among classical musicians mention should be made of the Hallelujah Chorus in Handel's *Messiah,* and among moderns mention may be made of Oliver Messiaen's *Quartet for the End of Time* (Theodore Presser, 1942). Nearer at hand is the hymnal and the text of such hymns as: "All Hail the Power of Jesus' Name"; "Holy, Holy, Holy"; "For All the Saints"; "Jerusalem the Golden"; "O Holy City Seen of John."

Scholars engaged in the discipline known as the philosophy of history have found in early Christian apocalyptic categories of thought highly relevant to their concerns. Many of them place high on their reading list Augustine's *City of God,* a profound effort to deal with the crises faced by the early Roman empire. That book remains one of the excellent expositions of the central thrust of the book of Revelation.

A comparable crisis in contemporary Western civilization is the focus for thought in William Stringfellow, *An Ethic for Christians and Other Aliens in a Strange Land* (Waco, Tex.: Word Books, 1973). This author finds the prophetic categories like Babylon and Jerusalem, death and the devil, to be necessary tools for dealing with current issues in ethics and politics.

Sermons on texts from the book of Revelation flow steadily from the presses, some good and some bad. I have not included any book of sermons. However, one of the ablest preachers of recent decades was Daniel T. Niles of Sri Lanka. In many of his sermons one may detect echoes of the Apocalypse, but especially helpful is his study *As Seeing the Invisible* (New York: Harper, 1961). This book shows how the activity of preaching has contributed to exegetical understanding.

The most extensive survey of scholarly treatments of the book of Revelation, a bibliographical survey of the literature available in all the European languages, is André Feuillet, *The Apocalypse* (New York: Alba House, 1965).